"A Climb to the Top *teaches career climbers how to become exceptional communicators. It is refreshing to see a credible sales leader provide the 'how-to' aspects via his 'Ten Commandments of Great Communicators.' This isn't just another business book . . . it's a hands-on, career Bible that you'll refer to again and again!"*

Alan Geller
managing director, AG Barrington, Inc.

"This profound book reaches into the core of human influence. As a leadership consultant myself, I am constantly looking for ways to inspire other people to achieve greatness. This book is a powerful blueprint for any leader striving for excellence!"

Dr. Matthew Miraglia
president, Matthieu Enterprises

"I have had the distinct honor of attending Chuck Garcia's seminars as well as collaborating professionally and academically at Mercy College. The central theme that runs through everything Chuck does, simply put is, 'It's not what you say but how you say it that makes the difference.' The demand for excellent communication is a fundamental requirement for virtually all professionals. Every message you convey could be a real opportunity to enhance and support your personal brand and that of your firm. Instant access to technology has profoundly changed audience expectations and behaviors. A speaker's words are going to be repeated, sometimes broadcasted, and often critiqued immediately, so the stakes are always high. Chuck's multidimensional, interactive communication model will provide you with the tools to enhance your personal brand, build a strong connection with your audience/constituents, and create effective communication strategies that both inspire and persuade.

A Climb to the Top *is a must-read for even those who think they're excellent communicators. Chuck Garcia delivers specific techniques and tools for speakers to use to develop well-crafted and concise messages with clearly defined objectives. His cutting-edge ideas will help you climb to the top. This book will certainly change how you think about yourself as a communicator, how you're perceived and measured by what you say and how you say it, and how to better navigate through the rough terrains as you climb to the top."*

Dave G. Kutayiah
senior vice president of human resources, Clarion Partners, LLC

"As a sales professional, Chuck is the greatest inspiration in my life. Effective communication skills are vital in both a successful career and life. A Climb to the Top is a must-read for any individual, as his message is captured in a unique, exhilarating, and memorable way."

Sean Robinson
sales development representative, Lever

"Chuck Garcia trained me in his 'Ten Commandments of Great Communicators,' which sparked a personal transformation to become a successful professional at a Fortune 50 company in under two years. I can say with confidence that the skills I acquired from Chuck's training are the main reason for my success."

Anthony Sicuranza, Jr.
executive compensation analyst, PepsiCo

"As a product of what Chuck demonstrates in this book and the classroom, I know that this book will change lives. A Climb to the Top provides readers with the recipe to go beyond their own expectations and beat the odds through the art of communication."

Christian Perez
operations analyst, Morgan Stanley

"As a physician-communicator, A Climb to the Top teaches the communication skills required to succeed in the current competitive business environment. Chuck's 'Ten Commandments of Great Communicators' has been life changing for me, allowing me to articulate my message to both patients with complex problems and our radio audience seeking insight on health and wellness. Collaboration with Chuck over the past thirty years has allowed me to witness firsthand the communications skills he has sharpened over the years and shares with his readers. As you climb with Chuck, he is by your side traversing you to the summit of success."

Joseph S. Galati, MD
host of Your Health First radio program; Liver Specialists of Texas

"We retained Chuck as our corporate sales trainer in order to elevate the skill set of our diverse sales and client services workforce in our NY office. Chuck used his 'Ten Commandments' as the foundation for the sessions in addition to customized sales techniques and methodology to reinforce the learning experience. Our sales force has embraced what they learned from Chuck, and we have seen an increase to our bottom line as a direct result. With his magnetic personality and powerful communication, Chuck engaged the audience and coached them to a higher level of communicators."

Scott Barrie
managing director

Niki Lee
VP of human resources, Trepp, LLC

"How does a young professional gain an advantage in such a competitive and fast-paced world? Leveraging Chuck's 'Ten Commandments' will equip you with the tools to become unique, stand out from the crowd, and take your career to new heights."

Ryan Chand
Fordham University

"Anyone looking to advance his or her career should read A Climb to the Top. *If you are looking for a career change or greater success in your current role, learning and practicing these communication skills is imperative."*

Tom Waldron
vice president of sales, EDR

"As engaging as it is insightful, A Climb to the Top *combines historic truths with modern techniques to help you advance your message and win over your audience.*

Whether you're an executive preparing a presentation for a board meeting or a college student trying to overcome a crippling fear of speaking in front of classmates, A Climb to the Top *is a must-read for anyone wanting to become a more persuasive communicator. Chuck's conversational prose and engaging style will leave you excited and prepared for your next presentation.*

From harnessing the power of a well-told story to seeing the benefit of speaking without a podium, each chapter is packed with irrefutable principles brought to life by clear and illustrative examples."

William Dodd
University of Texas at Austin

"Chuck deeply understands the vital link between compelling communications and driving business results. Every aspiring business manager who wants to build credibility with their clients and teams needs to read A Climb to the Top.*"*

—Brenton Karmen
global head of terminal sales, Bloomberg

"Under his mentorship, I have seen the transformation of his students who emerge looking, acting, and speaking like leaders. His spirit as a professor is one of a top artisan with a singular focus on the perfection of his craft, and each of his lectures bears his unique signature."

Dr. Ed Weis
dean, Mercy College School of Business; former managing director, Merrill Lynch

"I have been privileged to know Chuck Garcia his whole life. A Climb to the Top *is, like its author, eminently helpful, practical, and thoughtful. After a remarkable career building teams and helping top Wall Street firms succeed, Chuck is now turning his skills to helping others make the journey themselves. Every page of this book has something that will help you build trust, inspire loyalty, and lead effectively. It is chock-full of tips, techniques, and tactics, all told in a compelling and accessible way. I have already made it required reading for my students and clients. I know you will get a lot out of it."*

Helio Fred Garcia
author, The Power of Communication: Skills to Build Trust, Inspire Loyalty, and Lead Effectively; *executive director, Logos Institute for Crisis Management and Executive Leadership; adjunct associate professor of management and communication, NYU*

"*Chuck Garcia is a gifted salesperson, coach, and communicator. I was very fortunate to have a chance to learn from him firsthand while we were working together in financial technology. His book,* A Climb to the Top, *has taken many of his best lessons and distilled them down to their essence, giving you tricks, tools, and skills that will help you communicate with greater clarity, impact, and credibility. Whether you are marketing to the Fortune 500, raising money for your startup or—most difficult of all—attempting to convince your ten-year-old daughter to finish her piano practice,* A Climb to the Top *is a must-read for anyone looking to gain influence and change behaviors."*

Dave Zweifler
end-to-end lending solutions marketing leader, D+H

A
CLIMB
to the
TOP

A

C L I M B

— *to the* —

TOP

Communication & Leadership Tactics
to Take Your Career to New Heights

CHUCK
GARCIA

Advantage®

Published by Advantage, Charleston, South Carolina.
Member of Advantage Media Group.

ADVANTAGE is a registered trademark and the Advantage colophon is a trademark of Advantage Media Group, Inc.

Printed in the United States of America.

ISBN: 978-1-59932-688-7
LCCN: 2016932138

Book design by George Stevens.

This publication is designed to provide accurate and authoritative information in regard to the subject matter covered. It is sold with the understanding that the publisher is not engaged in rendering legal, accounting, or other professional services. If legal advice or other expert assistance is required, the services of a competent professional person should be sought.

Advantage Media Group is proud to be a part of the Tree Neutral® program. Tree Neutral offsets the number of trees consumed in the production and printing of this book by taking proactive steps such as planting trees in direct proportion to the number of trees used to print books. To learn more about Tree Neutral, please visit **www.treeneutral.com.** To learn more about Advantage's commitment to being a responsible steward of the environment, please visit **www.advantagefamily.com/green**

Advantage Media Group is a publisher of business, self-improvement, and professional development books and online learning. We help entrepreneurs, business leaders, and professionals share their Stories, Passion, and Knowledge to help others Learn & Grow. Do you have a manuscript or book idea that you would like us to consider for publishing? Please visit **advantagefamily.com** or call **1.866.775.1696.**

This book is dedicated to Frederick C. H. Garcia, my dad and the best teacher I ever had.

Contents

Foreword

by Dushyant Shahrawat

I t was October 1999, the height of the Internet boom, and I was at the Le Meridien hotel (now the Langham) in Boston listening to a splendid speaker talking about Bloomberg's position in the market and giving listeners a firsthand account of how Internet technology was impacting financial markets. When I asked someone who the impeccably dressed, well-spoken, and impressive speaker was, I was told he was Chuck Garcia, a well-recognized Bloomberg marketing executive. Little did I know that in time, we would become good friends, get to know each other very well, discover that we had a very similar upbringing living amidst the military, or that seventeen years later, I would be writing the foreword to Chuck's first book on a topic so dear to both our hearts and about which he has tremendous advice to offer.

I have two decades of experience in financial services, having worked at financial institutions, technology firms, and for the last decade as an analyst covering Wall Street and the investment industry. I've been privileged to speak at thought leadership events across twenty countries. I have been widely quoted in the press, interviewed on TV, and been a Fellow at MIT's Sloan School of Management. After interacting with innumerable executives and business leaders, I have learnt that effective communication is the prerequisite of great leadership and of professional success. Furthermore, good communication skills are not only vital for a successful career, but they also greatly improve personal relationships and enrich your soul. You see, we think people judge us by our *intentions*, but they actually judge us by our actions and words—by our ability to *communicate*.

I applaud you for taking the time to read this book, and I promise it will be a serious investment in your future. Let me also assure you that you can't have a better guide through this journey of discovery and self-improvement, than my friend Chuck Garcia. He is one of those rare individuals who possesses a blend of enormous experience, deep insight, and great humility. This book is his gift to us all, sharing crucial lessons of effective leadership and communication, skills he learnt and honed over a long and successful career.

Contrary to what you may think, effective communication is not God gifted or a natural-born ability but can be studied, practiced, and mastered. This is especially true for public speaking, as many examples in this book describe. Chuck does a remarkable job of making the tips, tricks, and tactics of public speaking accessible to all of us, and I urge you to take serious note of this book's valuable lessons, which will guide to becoming an exceptional communicator.

Authors write books for many reasons, but Chuck's motivation is special. It is a deep desire to share his wisdom with us all, to give back—especially to younger people—crucial lessons he has learnt about leadership, communication, and public speaking.

Please read on, and enjoy ascending the mountain with Chuck . . .

Acknowledgments

This book could not have been written without the loving support of Fran and the inspiration drawn from Harrison, Leigh, Garrett, and Gabby. Also, to call Peter Gianopulos an editor is insufficient. Thanks, Peter, for being such a great partner on this journey.

Introduction

*"It is the ultimate wisdom of the
mountains that a man is never more
a man than when he is striving
for what is beyond his grasp."*

—James Ramsey Ullman, climbing historian

May 28, 1953. It was twenty-five degrees below zero Fahrenheit. Altitude: 27,500 feet. Two men, Edmund Hillary, a beekeeper from New Zealand, and Tenzing Norgay, a mountaineer from Nepal, pitched a tent in preparation for their next milestone. The following morning, after a freezing, sleepless night, they left high camp and proceeded to climb. Fighting through snow, winding along a ridgeline with drops of over 3,330 feet on either side, they scrambled up steep, rocky steps and navigated a sloping snowfield on their way to the world's highest peak.

Wedging himself into a crack in the mountain face with the summit in sight, Hillary inched himself up to what was thereafter known as the Hillary Step. He threw down a rope, and Norgay followed. At 11:30 a.m. on May 29, 1953, the climbers stood on the top of the world and did what eleven prior expeditions failed to do. They achieved what had been considered the unachievable. Since that historic day, more than four thousand people have scaled their way 29,035 feet above sea level to the summit of Mount Everest.

You can watch a recreation of this event in *Beyond the Edge*, a 2013 docudrama about their monumental ascent. The event stunned the world and inspired many people to seek goals beyond their wildest imaginations. The story is about ordinary people achieving the extraordinary. It's also a lesson on cause and effect, risk and reward, conflict and triumph. Asked about the significance of this remarkable accomplishment, Hillary humbly said, "It's not the mountain we conquer but ourselves."

If you watch this or any other film on the topic, you'll notice the journey begins at a place called base camp. It's a staging area to assemble supplies, bond with your team, and mentally prepare for the challenges ahead. Ready to confront your fears and embark on the unknown, this feels remarkably similar to a career ascent.

Mountains are not climbed alone; neither are careers. They depend on the generosity you're willing to extend to your colleagues, known as the Law of Reciprocity.

It's a universal understanding to explain that in order to create success, extend help to others along the way. They in turn will assist and inspire you to reach your career summits.

Careers and Climbing:
Three Commonalities

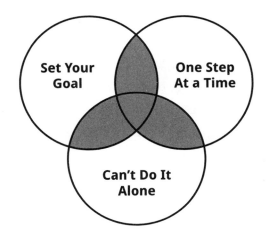

Mountaineering is also a metaphor for the way we climb the corporate ladder. In both cases, we set a goal, take one step at a time, and collaborate our way to the top. We bring our own ability, motivation, and mind-set on the way up. Having worked in high-performance cultures, one other observation about career climbing became evident. No matter what your job is, success will be determined:

- 5 percent by your academic credentials;

- 15 percent by your professional experiences;

- 15 percent by your natural ability; and

- 65 percent by your communication skills.

As a leadership-communication coach to organizations worldwide, my mission is to help people exceed their own expectations. While there are many ways to develop these capabilities, my approach is to take the wisdom, tactics, and approaches related to persuasive communication I've learned over the years and impart those skills to others.

The goal is to set high expectations for clients and students, challenging them to push out of their comfort zones. The character John Keating, played by Robin Williams in the movie *Dead Poets Society*, is my role model. He encouraged his students to be authentic, innovative, and to find the courage to plot their own career paths. I work to embody the timeless core values expressed by the Keating character, which remain as compelling today as they were when the movie was released in 1989.

- *We must constantly remind ourselves to look at things in a different way.*

- *No matter what anybody tells you, words and ideas can change the world.*

- *Strive to find your own voice because the longer you wait to begin, the less likely you are to find it all.*

Despite evolving management theories, differing corporate cultures, and various product lines, there is one common thread that weaves its way through today's economy: the top jobs go to the most compelling communicators. By committing to learn and apply the Ten Commandments of Great Communicators, the foundation of this book, you have taken the first step on your journey to the summit.

Climbing and public speaking also underscore the battles we fight in our minds as we seek to define the meaning of success. They tap into the deepest understanding of ourselves and help us realize the importance of tenacity in pursuit of success. As General George Patton once said, "I don't measure a man's success by how high he climbs but how high he bounces back when he hits rock bottom."

As you learn to apply these principles, many will seem unnatural, uncomfortable, and awkward. Public speaking brings fear and frustration to many. Rarely do these skill developments happen spontaneously. Like climbing a mountain, your ability to speak powerfully brings a new set of struggles. In both cases, it's in the act of overcoming challenges where professional and personal growth occurs.

Consequently, this book is not just about communicating or climbing your metaphorical mountains. It's about you and your success—and the recognition that it's rarely a straight line to the top. You'll zig and you'll zag recognizing that these tools and tactics will help you to keep moving up.

Success	**Success**
What People Think It Looks Like	*What It Really Looks Like*

The book is also a series of "how-to" lessons and a call to action to learn these techniques and put them into practice. As you contemplate the challenges that lie ahead, look to the mountains for inspiration, and reflect on these wonderful words of wisdom to propel your career to new heights:

"Challenge is the core and mainspring of all human activity. If there's an ocean, we cross it; if there's a disease, we cure it; if there's a wrong, we right it; if there's a record, we break it; and, finally, if there's a mountain, we climb it."

—James Ramsey Ullman, climbing historian

Welcome to *A Climb to the Top*. It is a privilege to be your guide on this journey of self-discovery and professional development.

CHAPTER 1

Primacy/Recency Effect: Begin with the End in Mind

"How much does your life weigh?

*Imagine for a moment that you're carrying a backpack.
I want you to feel the straps on your shoulders. Feel 'em?
Now I want you to pack it with all the stuff that you have
in your life. You start with the little things: the things on
shelves and in drawers, the knick-knacks, the collectibles.*

*Feel the weight as that adds up. Then you start adding
larger stuff: clothes, tabletop appliances, lamps, linens, your
TV. The backpack should be getting pretty heavy now. And
you go bigger. Your couch, bed, your kitchen table. Stuff it
all in there. Your car, get it in there. Your home, whether
it's a studio apartment or a two-bedroom house. I want
you to stuff it all into that backpack. Now try to walk.
It's kind of hard, isn't it? This is what we do to ourselves*

on a daily basis. We weigh ourselves down until we can't
even move. And make no mistake, moving is living.

—Ryan Bingham, *Up in the Air*

P layed by George Clooney in the movie *Up in the Air*,
Ryan Bingham, a corporate downsizing expert, flies
around the United States to fire people. He's the kind of
businessperson who feels more at ease at an airport than
in his own home. In his quest to help these recently unemployed
people find new jobs, Bingham delivers a speech called "What's in
Your Backpack?"

The character argues that commitments and possessions slow us
down. Get rid of them, he says. We're better off without them. He's
not only speaking about material things but also our backgrounds,
prejudices, and past experiences. These can be more debilitating and
make it even harder for us to move ahead.

Think about that speech for a moment and what makes it so
memorable. Instead of opening his speech with a statement, he poses
a thought-provoking question. "How much does your life weigh?"
And then through the use of a metaphor—that brilliant symbol of a
backpack—he provokes his audience to think about their lives in an
entirely new way.

Every member of his audience can relate to Bingham's words
on a personal level. He knows, even before he delivers his speech,
that every person will answer the question he's posing in a way that's
uniquely meaningful to them.

He sets the tone with a great opening—provocation. Imagine yourself in the audience waiting for career advice, only to be surprised by what you hear. That's both a powerful and unusual experience for most audiences to encounter these days. Instead of boredom, there's interest. Most people's immediate reaction is, "Where is he going with this, and why does it matter to me?"

What Ryan Bingham is asking us to do is technically impossible. Weigh our life? How? Why? You can only put so many things in a backpack. It's a great metaphor. He is delivering the unexpected and therefore grabbing our attention in the first fifteen seconds of his speech.

He is also providing insights about the way our brains work. He knows what an audience can absorb, and he's setting the stage for what ultimately will be a strong call to action.

The primary objective for anyone who delivers a speech is the same, regardless of the situation or objective. You strive to win the battle for the hearts and minds of your audience. That's the responsibility of any speaker, presenter, or leader—to inspire, persuade, and most important of all, provoke change.

George Clooney's character is letting us in on a trade secret. If you want to prepare for a speech the right way, begin with this fundamental assumption. Every time you step up to a dais, you should expect that:

- one-third of your audience views you favorably;
- one-third of your audience finds you unfavorable; and
- one-third of your audience is quickly waiting to make up their minds by hearing your first few sentences.

I'm certain the last third of the audience will nod their heads in all the right places. But if you don't play your cards right, their hearts and minds will drift somewhere else entirely, instead of focusing on what you're saying up on stage.

Coming to grips with this essential fact is one of the most critical keys to success. Why? Because it reminds you to remember that two-thirds of your audience is predisposed not to listen to you. They are there out of obligation, not choice.

It's your objective, therefore, to win over your audience in each and every speech you give, starting with the first words that come out of your mouth.

You have fifteen seconds to engage. Is it going to be "lift off" or "failure to launch"? If you look out over your audience early in your speech and you're not sure if you've hooked them, you've already failed. They're gone and not coming back.

If you don't start your speech with something that captures their attention, you're going to lose them immediately. And if you don't close with something equally compelling—an inspiring call to action that literally propels people out of their seats—you've basically wasted your time and theirs.

Open and close. First and last. Beginning and end. The Primacy Effect is all about what a speaker says first; the Recency Effect has to do with what he or she says last. All great communicators make lasting impressions by devoting a great deal of their attention to getting the bookends of their speeches just right.

Where should we begin? Let's start with the Primacy Effect.

THE ART OF MAKING A GOOD FIRST IMPRESSION: MASTERING THE PRIMACY EFFECT

People internalize the first things they hear, not what immediately follows. They perceive information presented early in a presentation as more valuable and meaningful than what comes next. So make your opening words count. Whatever you want to glue into the minds of your audience, say it first. Ask yourself, "If this were the only thing I would leave them with, what would it be, and why should they care?" And start there.

Before you speak, set the tone. Look confident. Start from a platform of conviction, and you have a shot at drawing them in and keeping them there.

Think about the two minutes you usually reserve at the start of your speech to offer friendly introductions, restate the obvious, or banter with your colleagues. Contrary to the conventional wisdom that expects you to thank your host and welcome the audience, save it for afterward. Then consider a different starting approach.

The people in the audience are too polite to say this—or show it—but they dread bland pleasantries. They'll smile and shake their head with affirmative nods then tune you out before you even get started.

Try something different. Startle them. Surprise them. Give them something to ponder. Say something controversial and provocative. The goal is to pique their interest while building your own credibility. Seek to establish a rapport by launching into something bold and memorable.

Consider using some of these opening tactics, which have proven to be highly successful for both my clients and me over the years:

Find an intriguing news headline. Audiences appreciate something timely that they can all relate to. Don't rely on celebrity stories; find something that has applicability to the people in the room. When Google announced it was changing the name of its parent company to Alphabet, I hooked my Wall Street audience by saying, "Let me tell you why they're doing this." If you're in a room with a sports crowd and something like the Tom Brady "Deflategate" scandal hits, use that. A trade association for textiles? Talk about a headline involving a fashion chain. The aim is to find common ground and then have people in the audience ask themselves the question, "Where is he going with this?"

Unearth a mysterious date. Don't lead with something like Sept. 11, 2001. Look for a date in history that will initially puzzle people. "The date was April 13, 1973. An event occurred that day that changed the world. It's a shame no one noticed. What happened?" You're building suspense as people start thinking to themselves, "I don't know what happened on April 13, 1973." If done well, they'll eagerly await the punch line. "At noon that day, on the corner of Lexington Avenue and 58th Street in New York, the first commercial cell phone call was made."

Tell a personal story. Be relatable right from the start. Showing your humanity and vulnerability will set the tone for everything that follows. "A funny thing happened to me on my way to this meeting. I was about to get on the train. I was on time, when the phone rang. In a rush I picked it up . . . only to discover that everything I thought I knew was wrong." People love it when well-accomplished speakers show their flaws and that they are just like them. Our "a-ha" moments often happen in unexpected places and at unpredictable times.

Open with a memorable quote. A famous quote from a well-respected or revered individual can help introduce your ideas in a way that provides the audience context about the topic at hand. For example, when I gave a presentation on "The Physicality of Student Engagement," I discussed how the academic model was broken and began with a quote from John Lennon: "When I was five years old, my mother always told me that happiness was the key to life. When I went to school, they asked me what I wanted to be when I grew up. I wrote down 'happy.' They told me I didn't understand the assignment. I told them they didn't understand life." Deliver the right quote, and you'll start to see heads nod in affirmation. You can just hear everyone in the audience saying to themselves, "You're right. I agree. That's so true!"

Go visual. You can build an air of mystery by rolling out a series of cryptic slides that lead an audience to an unexpected place. If you are speaking about the power of value investing, create a scene for a distinct and colorful introduction. Instead of an image of Warren Buffet, display a bottle of Heinz ketchup and a can of Benjamin Moore Paint. Put on an apron from the Pampered Chef, and hand everyone some peanut brittle from See's Candy.

These are not companies likely to be considered when someone plans to invest one million dollars of his or her own money. As we seek the latest and greatest technology company on our road to riches, these images help the audience understand that extraordinary investment returns can be accomplished through ordinary, everyday things. These companies are owned by Warren Buffet's Berkshire Hathaway and help explain his net worth of $66 billion. You found a fresh approach to introduce the concept of value investing and relied on a simple and straightforward way to make your points.

Those are just five techniques. There are many more. Develop your own based on your interests and the needs of the audience. They'll find it refreshing when someone deviates from the norm and starts with an approach that relates to them and their unique circumstances.

If you want to be remembered, do the opposite of what is normally expected. Find a way to engage them *before* you inform them. Build a rapport. Show your credibility. Establish a tone. Make everyone in the room say to themselves, "This guy cares enough about us and the issue at hand that he's thrown out the conventional approach and given us something new."

Information presented early in an opening statement acts as a lens of sorts that all subsequent information flows through. It's an opportunity to build your credibility. It's critical they believe you when the speech is over. Otherwise, you're just talking, not persuading. The starting point is getting them to listen—and then getting them to care.

URGENCY FROM STRENGTH: LESSONS FROM A MASTER COMMUNICATOR

I learned the importance of the first commandment chiefly from Lou Eccleston, the CEO of Canada's TMX Group. Lou is an inspiring leader who uses the Primacy/Recency Effect as a powerful tool and guiding principle to capture and sustain stakeholder attention. He is, quite simply, the best communicator I've worked with in my career.

When he took the helm of TMX in the fall of 2014, Lou observed an organization that was stuck in neutral and perceived as unresponsive to the needs of the marketplace. To strategically realign TMX, he knew that he needed to quickly get the attention of his employees.

"People are like pieces of human-direct mail," he told me. "You have a few seconds to get their attention. If you open up with everything is great, that's what they are going to hear. They stop listening right there." Like a direct-mail campaign, he recognized the need to grab his colleagues' attention quickly and follow with a captivating and memorable call to action.

To achieve his new objectives, Eccleston relied on his exceptional communication skills to achieve lasting cultural change. During the time he was with McGraw Hill Financial, he'd confronted similar challenges in his quest to drive brand value by collecting and integrating disparate assets. Although he had done this before, each situation has been different. When he moved to TMX, Lou called it "the transformational challenge of his life."

With the need for 1,400 employees to develop a mind-set of growth, responsiveness, and transformation, he used the Primacy Effect to set the tone. "TMX is a great company and its people work hard, but the situation is urgent," he told his team.

When Lou first arrived, he took the necessary time to thoroughly analyze the state of TMX's culture and highlighted some key takeaways:

- People weren't acknowledging that things were getting worse.

- Driven by their internal legacy, employees were locked in their old ways, inhibiting rapid response to the shifting financial industry landscape.

- They weren't listening to clients; they were trying instead to sell them products they neither needed nor wanted.

Fundamental to Lou's transformation was his ability to ensure TMX employees were driven by market and client demands. They then needed to change the way they thought, behaved, and acted. He firmly acknowledged they had great operating skills but needed to do a better job of spearheading lasting change. In short, TMX employees needed to develop exceptional communication skills. Effective communication is a bridge by which you travel across and find worth. "We were good at advocating but bad at communicating," he said. "There's a big difference."

Most regime changes in organizations of this size bring doubt and uncertainty—not, however, in a Lou Eccleston organization, which fosters candor and transparency. From his first day on the job, Lou firmly aligned words and actions. When asked about his leadership approach, his response was clear:

- I stand for simplicity—no hidden agendas.

- I'll listen to what you think, good or bad.

- I may not always agree with you, but I am going to take action and explain my rationale.

I've always admired Lou's ability to set a positive tone in spite of enormous pressure to exceed expectations. He once told me, "If you don't create urgency to change, people won't. It has to bring out the positive, otherwise you won't have any action." To maximize impact, Lou always ended his speeches with a direct address to his audience. They always walked away confident but also feeling that sense of urgency to enact change.

If you look at the opening and close of a Lou Eccleston speech, you'll see the power of the Primacy/Recency Effect. He starts with an attention grabber to communicate the reality of the situation and ends with an action plan and how he expects it to be executed. "The trend is bad," he tells his team, "but it's all grounded into how to fix the problems we've identified."

His message also provoked TMX to think about the business contrary to the status quo. "It's a different place than it used to be," he recently told me. "You can't stop changing if the clients are changing. You're out of step. Consequently, we don't have to be an exchange. From now on, we're a solutions company that happens to operate an exchange."

As I write this, Lou is focused on "must-have" products that support his client-centric, technology-focused business plan. It's all about what TMX can do for its clients. With ambitious growth plans, he's moved away from a broad diversification strategy and targets the development of technology-driven solutions that solve his clients' problems. His passion, energy, and laser focus are taking hold. The Primacy/Recency Effect is a fundamental tactic he continues to rely on to reinforce his message on the need to provoke organizational change.

While he aims to capitalize on growth in the quickly changing capital markets, Lou is confident his new vision and strategic direction will support a foundational philosophy he calls "urgency from strength."

Prior to his arrival, he felt the management of TMX was in denial that anything was wrong. Consequently, the foundation of his transformation is based on:

- **Awareness**—Intense competition is impeding revenue growth.
- **Conflict**—Admit we have a problem. Our clients are changing, and we're not keeping pace.
- **Resolution**—We need greater transparency, more effective communication skills, and accountability for our actions.

As Lou says, "You can run from it, or you can do something about it."

THE END IS ONLY THE BEGINNING: THE RECENCY EFFECT IN ACTION

When you're crafting your next speech, think for a moment about the shape of a hammock. The left-hand side of the hammock starts way up high. That's the opening of your speech, when your audience's attention is at its peak. Grab them or lose them. It all starts there.

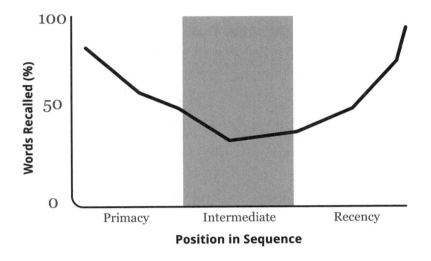

The middle of the hammock dips a little lower. That's the body of your speech. It doesn't matter how good a speaker you are; people's attention can't be sustained equally throughout an entire presentation. We don't have the ability to absorb all of the information that's coming at us with equal intensity. Recalling hundreds of words in a speech or a conversation is challenging under any circumstance. In conversational English, the average rate of speech for men is 125–150 words per minute.[1] Thus, we get fatigued, daydream a bit, and get lost in our thoughts.

But then comes the rise of the hammock again: the top part of the hammock on the right side. People can sense when a speech is coming to an end and tend to perk up. They begin to pay attention again. They want to know how it's going to end.

---

1   David Brooks Texas. "The Spoken Word: Today's tip for speakers." Last modified February 28, 2009. http://www.davidbrookstexas.com/blog-azine/category/the_spoken_word/.

Some of the strongest evidence to appreciate the importance of this phenomenon comes from a German psychologist named Herbert Ebbinghaus. He pioneered the experimental study of memory. One conclusion, known as the serial position effect, demonstrates that when participants are presented with a list of words, they tend to remember the first few and last few. They are more likely to forget those in the middle of the list. The Recency Effect applies to what is likely to be remembered at the end of a list of words.[2]

This is human nature. It's why movies start and end with a bang, why commercials begin with a hook and leave you with a price, and why concerts open and close with a band's best songs.

Leave people humming the right kind of tune. The conclusion of your speech is equally as important—if not more important—than your opener. The Recency Effect is subsequently your call to action—your chance to succinctly address the question as to why it was worth everyone's time to listen to your speech.

One of the biggest mistakes speakers make is that they don't signal that they are coming to the end of a presentation. They just talk right through it. As mentioned before, it's natural for people to perk up and pay attention at the close of your remarks, so let them know when you're approaching the end. Here are a few important techniques.

Summarize what has come before. Sometimes I summarize what I've said in my words, but occasionally, I ask audience members to condense what they think the key takeaways of my speech have been. Without disclosing

2   Kowalczyk, Devin. "Recency Effect in Psychology: Definition & Example." http://study.com/academy/lesson/recency-effect-in-psychology-definition-example-quiz.html.

it to the audience, you can call on a plant (someone you prepared prior to the speech to provide the summary). The dialogue with him or her acts as an "icebreaker" and works effectively to bring others into the discussion. Otherwise, call on an individual you don't know who has been paying close attention throughout the speech. Someone who makes frequent eye contact with you, sits on the edge of his or her chair, and is taking copious notes is a good target.

"Tell me, John Doe," I'll ask an engaged listener in the crowd, "from everything that you've heard today, tell me one takeaway that you've gleaned from this presentation."

John will likely say, "Here's what I'm thinking . . ." and communicate a few ideas.

By calling on people in the audience, you're showing that you want to involve others in your speech. You're asking them questions. You care about what they have to say. You want their opinion. People appreciate the effort and remember that long after the speech is over.

Use some stagecraft. Try asking a question but not answering it right away. "I've told you that we need to exceed our normal sales quota for this month. Can we do it?" Let the statement hang in the air for a bit. See what everyone's reaction is. Look around. Who's on board and who isn't? And then let that awkward silence work in your favor by urging people to ask themselves, "Why *isn't* he talking?"

Close the loop. Consider bringing your audience full circle back to where you started in some fundamental way. If you've opened with an unusual date or used a visual, try referencing your opening tactic in the close. It's a way to remind people of how you caught their attention earlier—which is a positive memory—so you can guide them to your next destination.

No matter what closing strategy you employ, it's imperative you leave the audience with a call to action—and provide them with something to do when they leave the meeting. Keep it simple. Don't use more than three bullet points to sum up what you want them to do, but propel them toward some kind of action.

The end of your speech is an opportunity to affect change—your chance to plant a seed and make it grow. Everything that you have said up to that point leads to your close. Inspire them. Help them see their own potential, and remind them of what you are asking them to do while it is still fresh in their minds.

Here's a great example. On September 12, 1962, in the height of the Cold War with the Soviet Union, President John F. Kennedy gave a speech on the campus of Rice University in Houston, Texas. On that day, using a rhetorical technique called the Rule of Three (to be explored later in this book), Kennedy emphatically stated:

There is no strife, no prejudice, no national conflict in outer space as yet. Its hazards are hostile to us all. Its conquest deserves the best of all mankind, and its opportunity for peaceful cooperation may never come again. But why, some say, the moon? Why choose this as our goal? And they may well ask why climb the highest mountain? Why, thirty-five years ago, fly the Atlantic? Why does Rice play Texas?

We choose to go to the moon. We choose to go to the moon in this decade and do the other things not because they are easy but because they are hard, because that goal will serve to organize and measure the best of our energies and skills, and because that challenge is one that we are willing to accept, one we are unwilling to postpone, and one which we intend to win."

Well, space is there, and we're going to climb it, and the moon and the planets are there, and new hopes for knowledge and peace are there. And, therefore, as we set sail we ask God's blessing on the most hazardous and dangerous and greatest adventure on which man has ever embarked.

And of course, on July 20, 1969, Neil Armstrong, an American astronaut from Wapakoneta, Ohio, set foot on the moon and uttered those famous words, "That's one small step for man—one giant leap for mankind."

President Kennedy's call to action inspired, persuaded, and provoked change. His words galvanized a nation to accomplish the impossible. Through effective use of the Recency Effect, President Kennedy left his listeners with a bold and memorable action plan. To amplify the speech's impact, he spoke with passion and purpose, instinctually moving Americans closer to his cause. Given the advent of the Cold War against the Soviet Union, he aroused the American people by infusing a strong sense of emotion into his address, which resonated long after his assassination.

When considering use of the Primacy/Recency Effect, begin your speeches with the end in mind. Tie your powerful, attention-grabbing opening together with a compelling and memorable call to action. Your goal is not only to compel your audience to listen. Your goal is to answer the question, "What do I want my audience to think, feel, or do, when this speech is over?"

CHAPTER 2

Emotional Appeal: Go for the Gold

When the United States Olympic hockey team glided onto the ice to face the Soviet Union in Lake Placid, New York, on Feb. 22, 1980, Cold War tensions had reached a boiling point.

A year earlier, the Soviets had invaded Afghanistan, rekindling simmering tensions between the two superpowers. The winner would advance to the finals to play for the gold medal, but there was far more at stake in upstate New York in 1980 than mere Olympic glory. The game came to take on a great deal of symbolic importance. It was Communism versus Democracy. Centralized Control versus Free Markets. East versus West.

Before the match, things looked bleak for Team USA. Having lost to the Soviets ten to three in a previous exhibition, the Americans were given zero chance of winning by the media and hockey pundits.

The Soviets were the most dominant team in the history of Olympic sports. With a win-loss record of sixty-two to six, they arrived at Lake Placid having won four straight Olympic gold medals.

The odds makers had them easily skating their way to a fifth. They practiced eleven months of the year and played with a remarkable unity of effort. The Americans were amateur college athletes, cobbled together by a combination of opportunity and circumstance.

Luckily, Team USA felt that this time they had an advantage. Their coach was an inspiring leader named Herb Brooks. A two-time Olympian himself, he was considered a "driven perfectionist" by his players. According to one of his players, "he treated us all the same, rotten." Some hated him; some loved him. But this much was undeniable: everyone on Brooks' team respected him. Still, hope for Olympic glory seemed beyond their grasp.

Fifteen minutes before the big game, Brooks walked into the locker room and came face to face with a team that looked as if it had conceded victory. Yet, he had a keen sense of situational awareness— an ability to take the pulse of his players by reading nonverbal cues. His players looked defeated, nothing more than a collection of slumped shoulders and vacant stares.

Knowing he had to capture their attention, he then did what great communicators do. He gave his team a call to action: win this game. But he did it in a way that relied more on emotion than reason. You can watch Brooks' speech depicted brilliantly by Kurt Russell in the movie *Miracle*.

In the film, the actor walks into the locker room, pauses for several moments and then says with tremendous confidence and conviction:

> *Great moments are born from great opportunity. And that's what you have here tonight, boys. That's what you've earned here tonight. One game.*

If we played them ten times, they might win nine. But not this game; not tonight. Tonight, we skate with them. Tonight we stay with them, and we shut them down because we can.

Tonight, WE are the greatest hockey team in the world.

You were born to be hockey players—every one of you, and you were meant to be here tonight. This is your time. Their time is done. It's over. I'm sick and tired of hearing about what a great hockey team the Soviets have. Screw 'em. This is your time. Now go out there and take it!

That's all he needed—just those 124 words delivered with passion and intensity. In that moment, Brooks gave birth to a locker room full of believers. When you watch the scene, you'll notice a few important techniques all communicators should remember when making an emotional appeal.

1. When Brooks walks into the locker room, he waits fifteen seconds before he says a word. He uses that silence to create dramatic effect to ensure he has their attention.

2. When he starts his speech, he begins with impact. "Great moments are born from great opportunity." He's in the moment. There is no past, no future. Just one game. "Tonight we shut them down because we can."

3. He ends with a call to action and emotional appeal that strikes a nerve with his team, which goes out and does exactly what he wants them to do—win that game.

If Brooks had appealed to his team's sense of logic, perhaps the game would have been over before it even began. Instead, he highlighted the opposite side of the same coin. He used emotion to move his team, which is one of the most important techniques that any communicator in any field should learn to make their own.

Want to move an audience to your cause? Or change their minds about a given topic? Or convince them to get out of their seats and buy something they swore they never would?

Then do what Herb Brooks did: appeal to your audience's base emotions, and you'll be able to move mountains.

EMOTION PRECEDES REASON

In *The Power of Communication,* Helio Fred Garcia, a well-respected crisis manager and phenomenal communicator, wrote, "Humans are not thinking machines. We're feeling machines who also think. We feel first, and then we think. As a result, leaders need to meet emotion with emotion before they can move audiences with reason."

Consider how we make decisions in our personal lives, and you'll see what Garcia means. Think about any businessperson trying to sell a new application that "will change the world." What does he need to say to someone to invest his or her time and listen?

Does he employ a logical argument? Does he bombard his prospect with facts, figures, and statistics? Not likely. Instead, he makes an emotional appeal. He expresses enthusiasm and passion and discusses why the application is so important to the prospect.

It is emotion that guides the major decisions we make in our lives and careers—not facts and figures. In my experience, the same is true for an audience, both large and small. It's puzzling that many presenters focus their attention on the facts and leave emotion behind.

To appreciate the science behind the power of emotional appeal, consider the research of Antonio Damasio. A professor at the University of Southern California, his body of work on the neurobiology of mind and behavior centers on emotion, decision-making, memory, communication, and creativity. In his book *Descartes Error*, he argues that emotion plays a central role in social cognition. When confronted with a decision, emotions from previous related experiences affix values to the options we are considering. These emotions create preferences, which lead to our decisions.[3]

George Campbell, a Scottish philosopher, said it best in his 1776 book *Philosophy of Rhetoric*: "When persuasion is the end, passion also must be engaged." How then do you generate emotional appeal in a world that demands metrics and empirical evidence?

Here are three key principles to keep in mind when you prepare to stand and deliver:

- **Use emotional language.** "Great moments are born from great opportunity."

- **Develop vivid examples.** "Tonight, we are the greatest hockey team in the world."

- **Speak with sincerity and conviction.** "This is your time. Their time is done. It's over!"

---

3   Murray, Peter Noel, PhD. "How Emotions Influence What We Buy." *Psychology Today*, February 26, 2013. https://www.psychologytoday.com/blog/inside-the-consumer-mind/201302/how-emotions-influence-what-we-buy.

When using emotional appeal to provoke an action, ask yourself what you are trying to evoke.

- pride
- hope
- compassion
- fear
- anger
- guilt
- reverence

Consider your message and the response you want to elicit from your audience. Your words and manner should reflect the feelings you are trying to activate inside an audience's hearts and minds.

When moving listeners to your cause, don't substitute emotional appeal completely for evidence and/or reasoning. Build your persuasive arguments around some degree of logic, but also seek to achieve the impossible by weaving emotion into that same appeal.

MAKING THE SALE: ERIC BERNSTEIN AND EMOTION AS A TOOL FOR PERSUASION

The great marketing agencies of the world figured this out long ago. If they want someone to buy something, they increase the probability of getting them to make a purchase by appealing directly to their sense of emotion. Then, in order to feel better about that purchase, people support their decisions with logical justifications.

Think about the profession of sales. Whenever someone submits a business proposal to a potential buyer, what he or she is really trying to do is to get the other party excited about the prospect of that purchase.

Imagine you're selling a machine. The machine performs some task faster than any other machine. That assertion is factual. But merely communicating your machine's lightning-fast processing abilities often isn't convincing enough to close the sale.

Good salespeople highlight the benefits of speed. They communicate how faster speeds can help a client solve a given problem. There is emotion wrapped up in that appeal. You're saving people time, effort, or helping them make money. And those solutions help get them excited about the future given the desire to improve their clients' bottom line.

It's a speaker's ability to make an audience feel something that eventually closes the sale. People, both in their personal and professional lives, make decisions that they feel are the right things to do rather than simply the logical things to do.

Take, for example, Eric Bernstein, the chief operating officer at eFront, a leading provider of software solutions to the financial industry. I saw Eric give a speech in 2008, right as the financial crisis was gaining traction, during an industry event where a dozen speakers were on the agenda.

While speakers that day stood behind a lectern and blandly discussed risk management metrics and bar charts, Eric did the opposite. Like a great actor about to deliver a command performance, he approached the spotlight with zeal and confidence and packed a wallop, earning both thunderous applause and rave reviews.

His presentation spoke to the audience's aspirations. He passionately discussed their concerns and helped them to understand how the appropriate risk-management software was not only a defensive tool for recovery but also an offensive weapon for profitability. It was a perfect blend of "I feel your pain" and "we'll get through this together." It was an emotional call to action, delivered at a time when people seemed to need it the most.

Bernstein's secret? "It's shocking to me how important emotion is in our business," he later told me. "I want the client to feel that I am not just a software vendor; I'm their partner. The majority of my job is to transform something from whatever it *is* to what I want it to *be*. Ninety percent of that is the human element."

It's Bernstein's ability to communicate emotion that has allowed him to successfully convert countless prospects into clients at eFront. "I'm a body language guy," Bernstein says. "I'm a psychology guy. You can always sense where someone is. You have to be able to pick up on that and determine when something is bothering them. It doesn't matter if it's on the job or in life, in a presentation or a one-on-one meeting. It starts and ends with their emotions."

When Eric meets a prospect, his initial interaction with him or her is often met with descriptions like *interesting* and *intriguing*. From the onset, he asks questions, starting with how his prospects do their jobs. In the middle of a response, Eric has been known to stop them dead in their tracks. "I tell them, 'I'm not interested in what you do,'" says Bernstein. "They (often) look at me funny, and (then) I say, 'I'm more interested in what you want to do. I want to know the ideal; what you're looking for.' I focus on what is meaningful to the guy on the other side of the table."

To translate those soft skills into running a profitable business, Eric believes in never diminishing the value of the product he's selling. When negotiating, it's easy to drop your price and be done with it, he says. But, the key to success often lies in a salesperson's ability to believe as strongly in the solution being sold and the value it provides as the person sitting across the table.

If you can find a way to communicate that trust in an authentic and emotional way, you do more than sell a product; you forge enduring bonds. As salespeople, there will be situations when you need to make a sale but may not feel as emotionally invested in that particular product compared to others. I recognize it's challenging to bring equal measure to everything in your suite. In spite of that, "Find a way to bridge the relationship to make it personal and provide that extra emotional touch," Bernstein says. "It's critical to drive business. To be fair, I like to think that when people meet, interact, and transact with me, ultimately they're building a friendship as well. To me, that's everything."

REMOVING THE CORPORATE MASK

After I speak with Eric Bernstein, I am often reminded of a great quote by the poet Maya Angelou, who said, "People will forget what you say, people will forget what you do, but they will never forget how you make them feel." When you're up on a podium, consider the spirit of Angelou's statement. Remember that people won't be able to recall the precise words you deliver or the exact way you present your ideas, but they will reflect on the way you make them feel.

After all, how often do you hear someone say, "I'm just not *feeling* it?" In order to make an audience feel your emotions, give them some part of yourself that is authentic and real. Peel away your mask, especially if you want to make your mark in the corporate world where everyone is expected to wear a facade of some kind. And then show them who is behind the veil.

I encourage my clients to think like a medieval knight. During the Middle Ages, when knights jousted, they wore helmets covering their faces. Before they jousted, dueling knights would lift up their visors and expose their faces to the crowds. This move gave birth to our modern-day salute, in which we raise our hands above our eyebrows. But what it really did was show onlookers who the man behind the mask really was.

The most successful communicators in the corporate world are those who can remove their masks. They show who they really are and relate to their audience by revealing their humanity.

And how do you do that? One of the ways is to share your failures. Revealing vulnerabilities is an effective way to strip away your mask and help people understand that you're just like them. You've had challenges. You've tried things. You've failed.

In other words, it's not always a straight line to the top. On a climb in the Andes, my team and I were on our ninth day of climbing. Less than four hours from the summit, I fell through a crevasse. While everyone on the team was safe, this eliminated our opportunity to reach the summit and caused us to adjust our methods to continue climbing safely. Not unlike careers, we sometimes fail to reach the goal in spite of our best efforts. We are vulnerable to events we can't always control. Also, it's the great leaders of the world that are able to show some vulnerability and say, "It hasn't always been easy."

If you can help an audience member see you as just another regular Joe or Jane who faced challenges, overcame them, and found success, you increase the chances to make a personal and lasting connection.

THE HEAD AND THE HEART: A STEVE JOBS PARABLE

For a master class in how to sell an idea—and in this case, a product as well—with emotion, watch Steve Jobs' June 12, 2005 Stanford commencement address. It's one of the most moving and effective pieces of oratory I've ever seen.

During the speech, Jobs talked about something powerful. He discussed the tremendous amount of time that we spend working at our jobs. If you're going to spend that much of your life doing one thing, he told his audience, don't you want to do work that matters?

He also gave the Stanford 2005 graduating class a great piece of advice. He said, "For the past thirty-three years, I have looked in the mirror every morning and asked myself, if today were the last day on my life, would I want to do what I am about to do today? And whenever the answer has been no for too many days in a row, I know I need to change something."

Jobs' call to action at the end of his Stanford address was equally interesting. He said, "When I was younger I got great advice. Be foolish." And by that he meant, "be foolish and be hungry." Those are the two calls to action he left with his audience.

He showed vulnerability, which was palpable and powerful. He was reminding us about the importance of asking questions when you don't know the answers. He talked about how hunger and foolishness often lead to inquisitiveness and how that inquisitiveness yields drive, building qualities and intangibles inside of us that are so important that we can't even measure them.

Here was a man who often was the smartest guy in the room. But notice how he often camouflaged his intelligence with emotion when he spoke. When Jobs introduced the iPod, he didn't talk about hardware and software. He talked about the prospect of having a thousand songs in your pocket. It was delivered in language that was easy to follow, packed with emotion, and translated easily from speaker to listener.

Jobs' communication tactics were straightforward. The smartest guy in the room did not communicate in facts and figures. He did so with simplicity, energy, and above all, conviction. When you integrate those three qualities—simple tones, creativity, and emotion—nothing is lost. They can absorb all of it, and the ideas behind your speech will stick.

For members of the audience, there is often a tug-of-war that is fought between their intelligence and their hearts. They feel one thing, but their minds tell them to do another. Most speakers start with the mind and try to get to people's hearts. I encourage my clients to do the opposite. Reach people's hearts first, and their minds will inevitably follow.

CHAPTER 3

Speak with Conviction: The Courage to Commit

In case you hadn't noticed,

it has somehow become uncool

to sound like you know what you're talking about?

Or believe strongly in what you're saying?

Invisible question marks and parenthetical (you know?)'s

have been attaching themselves to the ends of our sentences?

Even when those sentences aren't, like, questions? You know?

Declarative sentences—so-called

because they used to, like, DECLARE things to be true, okay,

as opposed to other things are, like, totally, you know, not—

have been infected by a totally hip

and tragically cool interrogative tone? You know?

Like, don't think I'm uncool just because I've noticed this;

this is just like the word on the street, you know?

It's like what I've heard?
I have nothing personally invested in my own opinions, okay?
I'm just inviting you to join me in my uncertainty?

What has happened to our conviction?
Where are the limbs out on which we once walked?
Have they been, like, chopped down
with the rest of the rain forest?

Or do we have, like, nothing to say?
Has society become so, like, totally . . .
I mean absolutely . . . You know?
That we've just gotten to the point where it's just, like . . .
whatever!

And so actually our disarticulation . . . ness
is just a clever sort of . . . thing
to disguise the fact that we've become
the most aggressively inarticulate generation
to come along since . . .
you know, a long, long time ago!

I entreat you, I implore you, I exhort you,
I challenge you: To speak with conviction.

To say what you believe in a manner that bespeaks
the determination with which you believe it.
Because contrary to the wisdom of the bumper sticker,

it is not enough these days to simply QUESTION AUTHORITY.
You have to speak with it, too.

—Taylor Mali, "Totally like
whatever, you know?"

I couldn't agree more with Taylor Mali.

Mali and I certainly work in different worlds. He is a slam-poet who travels the country speaking in poetic rhyme, teaching workshops, and doing commercial voiceover work. And I work as a professional speaker and leadership coach in the corporate world.

Yet we both share an unwavering commitment to helping people speak with clarity and conviction in every arena of their lives. Mali's poem eloquently highlights the importance of identifying—as well as eliminating—the use of filler words to increase the chances of effectively communicating our intended message.

What are filler words? You hear them every second of the day. *They're sort of . . . like . . . totally . . . I mean . . . Um, uh . . . ya know . . .* the wishy-washy kinds of words that people unconsciously use to punctuate their speech, both at work and in social situations.

Good speakers, however, avoid filler words like the plague, knowing that they instantly and irrevocably erode one's credibility. Filler words are not definitive. They're weak. They completely diminish the power of the ideas you are trying to impart to your audience.

Here's proof. In a study[4] done with college students, participants were asked to describe how they perceive people who frequently say "um" and "uh." Not surprisingly, the students rated "um-ers" as the following:

- uncomfortable

- inarticulate

- uninteresting

- ill-prepared

- nervous

- monotonous

- unsophisticated

- lacking in confidence

Need I say more?

But using filler words is only one of many diction choices that can damage your standing as a speaker. The second-worst culprit? Weak and wavering words that undermine people's confidence in your abilities.

Here's an example of how using timid-sounding words can hurt your career prospects. It's the story of a recent college graduate named John, who'd been hired by an industry colleague of mine to integrate data from various departments and create aggregated reports for management.

In John's first week on the job, his boss asked him if a report he was working on would be ready by five o'clock p.m. John's response

---

4   Jamie L. Pytko and Laura O. Reese, "The Effect of Using 'Um' and 'Uh' on the Perceived Intelligence of a Speaker," *College of St. Elizabeth Journal of the Behavioral Sciences,* (Spring 2013): 1–21.

was, "It should be ready by five." His boss, c
John, "You know what? Let's hang up the pl
few seconds, and tell me that the report *will*

Think about the difference between tl
much confidence did the word *should* con_._,
munication? In my colleague's company, there is no room for u.._
tainty when it comes to report readiness. They are either on time
or not. The report had to be ready at five o'clock p.m. It was John's
responsibility to manage his boss's expectations. It's best not to leave
any doubt when ready to deliver.

That exchange proved to be a learning moment for John. Now,
as a matter of practice, he delivers his reports a few hours early each
week and eliminated words like "should" or "could." He has gained
his manager's confidence, who now knows that John says what he
means and means what he says. The best speakers communicate the
same confidence and conviction when they stand center stage.

Why would anyone follow you up a mountain, onto the playing
field, or into the line of fire if you use weak words? Why would people
buy what you are selling?

In order to become a leader, project strength. And that strength
should be communicated, first and foremost, via the quality of the
words you choose.

The overuse of filler words is not simply a problem for Generation X-ers and Millennials. Speaking with conviction is far more
than the absence of filler words. It is also expressed in actions and
reactions.

More than a century ago, the philosopher Thomas Carlyle said,
"Conviction is worthless unless it's converted into conduct." Ask most

preneurs about the start-up challenges they confront, and likely agree with Carlyle's base assumption.

Start-ups require the three Cs: courage, capital, and conviction. You need all three to succeed as an entrepreneur, but each works in different ways. Courage is felt, capital is raised, but conviction has to be demonstrated in order to be of value. Ask Mark Suster of Upfront Ventures what he looks for when investing capital with an entrepreneur, and his response is, "The defining factor of our internal decision process is *conviction*. I trust my partners to make hard calls on investment decisions because no decision to invest millions of dollars is easy."[5]

REFLECT, DON'T DEFLECT: ALEC GUETTEL AND THE COUNTLESS FORMS OF CONVICTION

Look at the way Alec Guettel, a serial entrepreneur who cofounded Axiom Law and redefined the practice of law, conveys his passion and beliefs, and you'll see how powerful conviction can be.

When it comes to dealing with investors, Guettel subscribes to a single golden rule. He never leaves a meeting without divulging— in one way or another—some of his own personal weaknesses. He's up front about what he doesn't know or has struggled to do well in the past. In fact,

---

5   Truster, Mark. "Why I Look for High Convention, not Consensus, in Venture Captial Decisions." September 26, 2015. http://www.bothsidesofthetable.com/2015/09/26/ why-i-look-for-high-conviction-not-consensus-in-venture-capital-decisions/.

he makes it a priority to show people his vulnerabilities, knowing that his honesty builds trust and long-term relationships.

He created Axiom, like every other venture he's launched, solely because he had an unwavering belief in the mission. Axiom's goal is to provide exceptional legal services at a fraction of the cost of conventional law firms. The company was built with his partner Mark Harris to upend the status quo and transform the historically static legal industry into something that disrupts the way services are rendered in the country's largest companies.

In the beginning, Axiom was simply two people sitting in a room intent on shepherding novel ideas into action, but there was an undeniable air of conviction in that room as well. Guettel and Harris looked for other like-minded believers who shared their general philosophies. Their conviction bred more conviction in part because everyone they brought onto the team was brutally honest with each other.

"We give each other feedback with authentic, grown-up communication," says Guettel. "If people can't handle that, we don't want them in our organization. This is a thing we call *reflect, don't deflect*. When you have feedback or complaints for someone—reflect it directly to them. Talk to them about it rather than deflecting it to others by complaining about them."

Visit the Axiom office in New York and you'll notice that each conference room tells a story about a particular lesson the company has learned over the years. On a table in their lobby is a small orange booklet that contains the fond and not-so-fond memories of the Axiom adventure so far.

On the surface, these might seem like stories of struggle and crisis, but when you listen to and read them, they're stories about the power of conviction—lessons about the importance of holding onto belief in the face of skepticism.

One of the booklet's stories describes an event that occurred in 2000 that underscores Axiom's power of conviction. Seeking to raise capital for funding needed to accelerate growth, Guettel and Harris met a variety of venture capitalists. Venture Capital (VC) plays an important role in a company's life when it begins to commercialize its innovation. In the final round of Axiom's founders first ever partner's meeting, the VC managing partner "uncorked a withering critique in the form of a question." Alec nearly dove under the table. Lacking any coherent response, in sheer desperation, Mark replied, "With all due respect, Joseph, you have no idea what you're talking about."

Joseph and his partners became Axiom's first VC investors. Sixteen years later, it is a thriving organization with 1,600 employees worldwide—fueled in large part by Guettel's and Harris's strongly held convictions and unique ability to persuasively communicate those beliefs to venture capitalists, clients, and employees.

The Axiom story is an example of businesspeople committed to an idea and an unwavering desire to provoke change. They refused to buckle down or diminish their ambitions in the face of uncertainty. Axiom embodies what Robert Kiyosaki, an investor and self-help guru said: "The keys to success, in business and in life, are truthfulness, the ability to take and give, honest and well intentioned feedback, strength of character, and conviction in one's principles."

Axiom illustrates that if we don't have confidence in our own words, why should our audiences have confidence in us? If we don't believe in the message that we are conveying, how can we hope to move others closer to our cause?

An article in *Nature Neuroscience* led by Benedetto De Martino, a cognitive neuroscientist in the field of decision-making and neuroeconomics, states that the brain has direct links between knowing what you want and the ability to express it.[6] His research demonstrated that the more confident a person was in his or her ideas, the more likely they were to maintain those beliefs over time. These deep-seated principles led to a capacity to speak with greater conviction.

Conviction does not guarantee success. But a lack of it almost always guarantees failure. It's a personal and deep seated belief that compels companies to move forward in spite of doubt and cynicism. Conviction drives decision making, promises action, tolerates risk, and overcomes doubt. It doesn't always always happen immediately but progresses over time through both positive and negative experiences. In many cases, it develops by observing the successes and failure of others.

Travis Bradberry, a leadership expert and co-author of *Emotional Intelligence 2.0.* said, "In business, things change so quickly that there's a great deal of uncertainty about what's going to happen next month, let alone next year. Leaders with conviction create an environment of certainty for everyone."

However, conviction is a balancing act that requires caution and care. It's a double-edged sword and can work equally for or against you. When training clients, I discuss an interesting set of precepts put forward by an influential Finnish communications theorist

---

6   De Martino B, Fleming SM, Garret N, and Dolan RJ. "Confidence in value-based choice." *Nature Neurosci.* January 16, 2013: 105–10. doi: 10.1038/nn.3279.

named Osmo Antero Wiio. He discussed how it's the listener's job to interpret our words. Like a powerful weapon, it is a valuable asset when used correctly and can cause self-inflicted harm if used inappropriately.

Wiio[7] asserted that there are three central truths to keep in mind when we communicate:

1. **Communication usually fails, except by accident.** The truth of the matter is that communication usually does fail. People who have poor communication skills have virtually no chance of having an audience understand exactly what they want to say. But even good communicators need a variety of factors to occur for the intended message to be perfectly absorbed by an audience.

2. **If a message can be interpreted in several ways, it will be interpreted in a manner that maximizes damage.** When you communicate an idea, particularly when you're giving a speech to hundreds of people, your audience is going to take the path of least resistance. People will interpret your words the way they want to interpret them. They will tell you what they think you meant instead of what you actually meant.

3. **There is always someone who knows better than you what you meant by your message.** Wiio asserts that the power is centralized in the listener, not the speaker. If you fail to convey what you're actually trying to communicate, then you weaken your call to action.

---

7   http://osmo.wiio.net/in-english/

I find these rules to be particularly insightful. As the following example illustrates, the power of conviction can work against you if not harnessed properly.

Sometimes the combination of a few spoken words can destroy an entire company in ten seconds. Imagine you say something and immediately want to take it back. But it's too late. The damage has been done. This is any speaker's worst nightmare and can happen to even the most successful businesspeople anytime, anywhere.

Known as the Ratner Effect, it's named after Gerald Ratner, the former CEO of a jewelry empire whose stores included Ratners, H. Samuel, Ernest Jones, Leslie Davis, Watches of Switzerland, and over a thousand shops, including Kay Jewelers. Although the chain was considered "tacky" by the press and other jewelers, its success turned Ratners into a billion-dollar business and became a household name throughout England in the 1980s.

On April 23, 1991, it all came crashing down in what seemed like an instant. On that day, Gerald Ratner gave a speech to a group of high-powered businessmen and journalists on how he grew a small family-owned business into an empire in a few short years. The speaking engagement, which Ratner himself now refers to as "the speech," is considered one of the biggest blunders in the history of business.

During the speech, someone in the audience asked him how he was able to sell things so inexpensively. His response: "We also do cut-glass sherry decanters complete with six glasses on a silver-plated tray that your butler can serve you drinks on, all for £4.95. People say, 'How can you sell this for such a low price?' I say, because it's total crap." He continued speaking and said earrings sold by the Ratner

Group were "cheaper than an M&S prawn sandwich but probably wouldn't last as long."

This perfectly illustrates Wiio's second central truth of communication, which states that listeners will interpret your words however they want, regardless of your intended meaning. Ratner claims the comments were taken out of context, and he thought that being at a private event, nothing he said would be reported to the public. By his own admission, Ratner was "inserting a bit of humor, as I often did." The journalists there thought differently and interpreted the comment as making fun of his customers. Although this was before the days of Twitter and Instagram, his comments were national news the next day. The hordes of previously loyal customers stopped coming almost immediately.

The effect on the company's profits was catastrophic. Almost overnight, shares in the company plummeted. As Ratner recounted in an article that appeared in the Daily Mail[8] in 2007, "That speech cost me my business, my reputation, and my fortune. I lost a £650,000 salary. I saw £500 million wiped off the valuation of my company and a billion-pound turnover slashed almost overnight."

They never recovered. Ratner sold a majority of the company's shares in an attempt to save his business but was subsequently fired by the company's new leader in November 1992. The company then changed its name to Signet Group in September 1993 to distance the newly led organization from the calamity that Ratner had caused.

The phrase "doing a Ratner" entered the English lexicon as a term that refers to self-inflicted harm that ruins reputations, and in some

---

8   Gerald Ratner, "Confessions of Mr. Crapner: How Gerald Ratner made a 24-carat mess of his life," *Daily Mail,* (November 2007), http://www.dailymail.co.uk/femail/article-491448/Confessions-Mr-Crapner-How-Gerald-Ratner-24-carat-mess-life.html.

cases, entire businesses. The Ratner Effect is proof that Murphy's Law is as applicable to communication as anywhere else. Anything that can go wrong with a given set of spoken words often will.

We all want to sound clear, definitive, and sure of ourselves, but when we speak, things sometimes go terribly wrong. Poor word choices spoken in the wrong order with inappropriate contexts can get us into trouble.

Conviction comes in many forms. It does not only appear in speech communication but also in conversations with colleagues, clients, and prospects. When you speak, choose your words carefully. As you learn the techniques of conviction on the podium, apply those same tactics in meetings and daily interactions.

While conviction can cause self-inflicted harm and ruin a company, it is also an essential ingredient to build a thriving organization capable of disrupting the status quo. Don't fear it. Use it as a tool for self-improvement and professional development. If you find yourself in a situation unsure of what to say, listen to the commands of Taylor Mali: "I entreat you, I implore you, I exhort you, I challenge you: To speak with conviction."

CHAPTER 4

Body Language: The Body Speaks before the Mouth Opens

"Your body will never be more connected to your mind than when something is at stake. That's how you measure the value of a moment, by its consequences."

—Erwan Le Corre, fitness enthusiast and leading educator of MovNat, a physical education and fitness discipline

I t happens often. When you give a speech, someone else, usually a master of ceremonies, introduces you to the audience. He or she discusses your background, states some of your accomplishments, and says, "Please welcome John Smith to the podium."

Immediately after the introduction, you stand there facing the audience. You haven't said a word, and yet you usually hear hands clapping. Audiences, by and large, are generous with their applause. Although you haven't earned their praise yet, they tend to welcome you with warmth and fanfare.

And then it comes. *Pause. Pause. Pause.* Those are the three seconds of silence between their fading claps and the first words of your speech. What's happening during that short transition? It's clear; people are sizing you up.

It happens every time you get up on stage. Without exception, audience members will look at the way you are standing, your clothing, your eye contact, and your bearing. They are making personal judgments.

Do you appear trustworthy? Competent? Confident? What kind of vibe are you projecting? Are you someone to approach or avoid? All this is based upon the nonverbal cues you give to your audience.

Many speakers spend hours honing their scripts, seeking to choose exactly the right words, only to pay little or no attention to the visual judgments that audiences are making about them when it's time to stand and deliver.

That's a mistake. In the 1960s, Albert Mehrabian of UCLA did extensive research to understand the order of magnitude of verbal versus nonverbal communication. In his book *Silent Messages*, he asserted that:

- 55 percent of communication is nonverbal—your bearing;

- 38 percent is vocal—the manner in which you engage; and

- 7 percent are words—choose carefully.

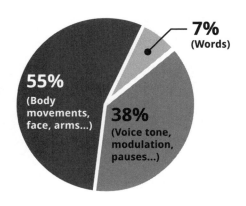

7%
(Words)

55%
(Body movements, face, arms...)

38%
(Voice tone, modulation, pauses...)

These judgments are being made at lightning speed. In fact, my own research suggests that people make decisions about you in the first seven seconds they see you. And it's these early judgments that often prove to be one of the key predictors as to whether your speech will be perceived positively or negatively.

How do you avoid negative first impressions? Step one is to take stock of what you look like in the mirror. Don't be overly critical of your appearance, but be objective. Did you cut yourself shaving? Are you wearing a suit that doesn't quite fit right anymore? Having a bad hair day? It's best to adjust those, as minor as they may seem, before you step on stage.

Your effectiveness can be quickly inhibited if the audience is distracted and thinking that something is out of place. *His tie is too short. His button is unbuttoned. Her blouse is covered with lint.* Once an audience starts thinking about your appearance, they're likely not paying attention to your words but to the annoyance that caused the distraction.

Think about the great actor who steps on stage. People who carry themselves like they have a positive self-image—people brimming with optimism, hope, and confidence—tend to communicate those good feelings right along with their ideas. It often starts by thinking about your capabilities and talents, then having the courage to recognize you're going to make mistakes.

Everybody makes mistakes. The key is to learn from them and not make the same mistake twice. Don't strive for perfection. Strive for progress. Think in terms of increments. It's how you climb a mountain, a little bit at a time.

"LOOK THE PART TO GET THE PART": LESSONS FROM A TELEVISION SHARK

While you can't always judge a book by its cover, book-jacket and product-packaging designers have created a niche industry based on the notion that consumers indeed purchase products based upon how they look.

Like it or not, the clothes you wear make a strong visual statement about how you see yourself. Comfort may aid productivity, but in an era when we're all expected to be walking, talking brands, the decision to wear flip-flops, sweatpants, or jeans may not be the best way to dress for success.

You might think you're expressing your individuality, but you're also sending a message that you're not a serious professional—that you're not here for business. Appropriate dress is a way of expressing respect for the situation at hand as well as your colleagues.

When it comes to clothing, you'd better look the part or you might not get the part. That's the advice from Daymond John, an American entrepreneur, investor, television personality, author, and motivational speaker—a man best known as the founder, president, and CEO of a company called FUBU. He's also known for his appearances as an investor on the popular TV show *Shark Tank*.

As far as John is concerned, we should all dress strictly according to our profession and position—and always dress to kill.

John feels that this is the single-most important rule to follow in suiting up for each workday. I once read a memorable quote in a magazine article where John said, "Your look really needs to be true to your profession. Don't come as a construction worker dressed in silk. I need to see you in some overalls with a hardhat. If you're a coder in the tech world (and) you walk into the room in a nice three-piece suit, I won't believe that you're in a dark room for four days coding. I'm just not buying it. Always dress to what is accurate to who you are and what you are."[9]

John said that his rule is particularly applicable if you work in the financial arena. If you're in a suit that's not fitted and you have a bunch of jewelry on, John says most people will suspect you are loose with your money. We all make our own judgments between the way people look and the way we feel about their overall competence.

John subscribes to one fashion rule above all others. "We had a saying in the hood," says John, who was born in Brooklyn. "Just keep it real."

Nothing turns John off faster than a guy who misrepresents who he is. He's looking for authenticity. He said you can spend $6,000 on a Brioni suit, but if you look uncomfortable or it's not tailored right, it's going to hurt you.

Today, the middle-aged business icon, who could pretty much wear anything he wants and still command respect, continues to focus intently on what he wears. "In *Shark Tank*, I put a lot of conscious

---

9 Kim Lachance Shandrow, "The Stars of *Shark Tank* on How to Dress for Success," *Entrepreneur* (September 22, 2014) http://www.entrepreneur.com/article/237709.

effort into what I wear," says John. "My suit is always going to be edgier than the other Sharks, and I'd never wear cufflinks that big outside the studio. My tie is going to have a double Windsor with a fat knot, and I'll pick a color that's a little brighter. Not to show off but to represent myself in broad strokes."

John's ensembles are more understated when he's doing interviews on Bloomberg or CNBC. He says, "I wear a form-fitting pinstripe suit and a power tie. The different aspect of me is being represented. I'm there as a finance expert. On Shark Tank, I'm an investor with an expertise in lifestyle brands. My clothes have to represent that."

And the biggest fashion lesson he's learned from Shark Tank is the importance of fashion details. Not just the suit. People notice whether your nails are trimmed or if your shoes are shined. If you wear earrings like John does on the show, it might become part of your public image, whether that was your intention or not.

To quote John, "Everything matters. Everything."

THE FIVE CATEGORIES OF NONVERBAL COMMUNICATION

We make statements before we even say a word, not only in how we dress but with our posture and body language as well.

When I work with clients, I help them break down their individual nonverbal forms of communication into five categories.

It should be noted that four out of five categories are negative. The implication is that you have a greater chance of causing self-inflicted harm nonverbally than you do when you speak.

1.   AGGRESSIVE: closed

These postures tend to arise when speakers are unsure how to answer a question or when they try to project too prominently with their bodies.

- hands on hips

- invading personal space—too close

- aggressive gesturing—finger pointing

- standing over someone

- overly firm handshake

2.   DEFENSIVE: closed

When you think about the defensive posture, consider a boxer who uses his gloves to protect his face. His fists are up because he's about to get punched by someone in the nose.

- crossed arms or legs

- hunched shoulders

- poor eye contact

- leaning away

3.   NERVOUS: closed

Think about that moment, in the middle of a speech, when you feel a tickle in your throat. You start coughing—and just can't stop. You feel compromised and weak; you lose your power by striking these positions.

- nail biting

- dry throat—swallowing/coughing

- blushing—face/neck/chest

- weak handshake

- avoiding eye contact

4. BORED: closed

Avoid giving the impression that you are obligated to be there—that you're delivering your speech out of necessity instead of out of your own volition.

- looking around the room

- looking at watch

- drumming fingers

- yawning

5. INTERESTED: open

These are positive postures that project friendship, concern, or empathy. The more you can show people that you are listening to them or are interested in their ideas, the better.

- firm handshake

- good eye contact

- confident stance and gestures

- showing interest—head nod/slight lean in

- broad smile

THE DO'S AND DON'TS OF BODY LANGUAGE

Communicators who work on these postures create important visual cues for their intended audience. Once you are comfortable on how you project nonverbally, try to make your audience feel what you are feeling. Below are some techniques you employ in order to maximize your body language and be a more persuasive and effective communicator:

1.   **What you want to convey:** Many people call this your "vibe." You see it in musicians—the proverbial "rock star"

vibe. Before you begin a speech, whether you're walking into a boardroom or stepping on stage, think about the situation that you are in and make a clear choice about the attitude you want to project. Do you want to look powerful? Vulnerable? Confident?

2. **Where and how you stand in space:** Status and power are nonverbally conveyed by height and space. Standing tall, pulling your shoulders back, and holding your head straight are all signals of confidence and competence.

3. **How you approach others:** After a speech or a meeting—when the camera is off—is when the magic usually happens. You've given a speech, and if you provoked a reaction, someone is going to want to approach you. Smile. You're sending a signal that you are friendly and approachable.

4. **What your eyes are saying:** The eyes can be a window into your soul. If you are looking straight into people's eyes, it's very difficult for them to look away. They feel an immediate attachment and they look back. Try making a practice of noticing the other person's eye color, which is one way of staying focused. How often do you hear, "He didn't even look me in the eye"?

5. **How you shake hands:** It's the quickest way to establish rapport. It's what we use to reach out and say, "I'm pleased to meet you. What a pleasure." Shake their hand, not too tight, not too loose. It shouldn't be limp because that's what they're going to remember.

6. **What gestures you make:** Avoid looking rehearsed, like you're a trained robot. Use your hands when you are giving

a speech just as you would in ordinary life. Just be natural. Wherever your hands happen to end up, that's where they end up.

Every encounter—from conferences and meetings to training sessions and business lunches—is a unique opportunity to meet people, network, and expand your professional contacts.

Your gestures and body movements should convince those around you that you are lively and energetic. Bring your mind, body, and spirit to every encounter and audience engagement.

Making a positive first impression is critical. You have just seven seconds—but if you handle yourself in the right ways, seven seconds are all you need. If words are stripped away and the only communication left is body language, the truth will find its way to the audience. Before you stand and deliver, remind yourself that the body speaks before the mouth opens.

> Sian Beilock, PhD, is a psychology professor at The University of Chicago and one of the world's leading experts on the brain science behind "choking under pressure." In April 2012 she published an article called *The Fear of Public Speaking* that asserts that it's the threat of social evaluation that makes public speaking so nerve wracking.[10] Even if you come prepared to give a speech, why do some people lose their composure when put on the spot and others thrive? What is the right strategy to minimize nervous tension and maximize impact?

---

10   Beilock, Sian PhD. "The Fear of Public Speaking." *Psychology Today.* April 25, 2012. https://www.psychologytoday.com/blog/choke/201204/the-fear-public-speaking.

She states that for over twenty years, researchers have invited people into their laboratories to stress them out by asking them to prepare a speech and deliver it to others.

The goal is to determine what makes these situations so stressful and how to overcome the associated challenges.

The research described is based on the Trier Social Stress Test. Each study contributor enters a room, faces a three-member panel, and is asked to create a five-minute presentation. The goal is to convince the panel that he or she is the right candidate for a position in their laboratory. They have ten minutes to prepare and are told that their evaluation is based on content and presentation style.

With the video cameras rolling, each person stands and delivers. To add more stress, when the speech is over, they are then asked to count backward from 1,022 by 13 out loud as quickly and accurately as possible.

Beilock cites this research to underscore that public speaking is a "clear and reliable way" to elicit a stressful response. Yet, it's not only the act of giving a speech that causes the tension. The Trier Social Stress Test triggers anxiety because it includes elements of social evaluation. In other words, when people are judging you and your performance, speakers are afraid of being evaluated on the chance they may look foolish.

Her suggestion is to condition yourself to lessen the pressure that comes with public speaking. She concludes that if you spend a little time each week making a fool of yourself, that experience will help diminish the fear when you are ready to deliver. She recommends everyone take an acting or improvisation class. I couldn't agree more. With most of my clients and students I teach principles from a book called *YES, AND: How Improvisation Reverses "No, But" Thinking and Improves Creativity and Collaboration.* Based on lessons from The Second City, this idea is not just about developing comedic skills. You become conditioned to think and respond quickly on your feet. It helps you learn how to overcome the fear of public speaking in a nonthreatening and nonjudgmental way.

Beilock's research emphasizes that when you have already experienced the worst thing that can happen when you give a speech, you're less likely to stress out about it with each successive attempt. Eventually, you'll be so accustomed to scripted and spontaneous communication, that reducing anxiety will translate into a more confident public speaker.

CHAPTER 5

Minimize the Distance: Teach, Don't Preach

F ounded in 1636, Harvard University is the oldest institution of higher learning in the United States. Although never formally affiliated with a denomination, Harvard's primary aim was to train Congregationalist and Unitarian clergy. Their faculty educated students much the same way that professors and coaches teach today. They modeled the types of professional behaviors they needed to become persuasive ministers and preachers.

Their students were required to study Scripture and learn how to deliver religious sermons. Professors were tasked with teaching their students hard skills (bodies of knowledge) and soft skills (techniques for how to properly communicate that body of knowledge). Students were instructed to stand behind a lectern on an elevated pedestal, often positioned far from their congregants, and use their "platform" to pass their knowledge on to the masses.

They preached, professed, or otherwise instructed, while their congregation was expected to sit, listen, and absorb all of the wisdom being delivered to them from the pulpit. Given Harvard's success at training fine Christian gentlemen, this educational model gained traction quickly. Other institutions of higher learning followed and began modeling their own teaching methods after what was going on in Cambridge, Massachusetts.

Fast-forward to the present and you'll find that college lectures as well as speeches in the business world are often conducted in similar ways. A speaker stands behind a lectern, keeping plenty of distance from his or her students, while offering minimal audience engagement or interaction.

It's unfortunate. We are stuck in a conventional delivery rut that dates back to the seventeenth century. We're conditioned to believe that there should be barriers between a speaker and an audience. This is a time-honored tradition suitable for change.

Speech communication doesn't have to look and feel like a seventeenth-century sermon. Why rely on archaic traditions from a command-and-control era when we're living in an age of democratization and interaction?

Perhaps the communication models of the past weren't designed to ensure speakers could build a rapport or establish a personal connection with their audiences. Today, collaboration and connection have taken center stage. Our approach to speech communication should evolve along with societal expectations.

BECOME A KNOWLEDGE SPECIALIST

There was a reason why Harvard's professors taught their students to deliver sermons in a particular way. In the seventeenth century, knowledge was scarce. It was incumbent upon speakers to impart knowledge to their audiences. However, you can google almost any subject and quickly access basic knowledge.

Modern audiences tend to be interested in what the professional world calls "subject-matter expertise." That's a formal way of saying that the world craves specialized knowledge.

Medical science is a great example. In the past, if you went to see a doctor, you'd see a general practitioner. Now, we see specialists: cardiologists, gastroenterologists, endocrinologists, and the like. It's the same in finance. There are discrete disciplines in which speakers are expected to have expert knowledge. From mortgage-backed securities to mergers and acquisitions, the world continues to demand specialization from industries worldwide.

Consequently, in terms of content, that's where speakers can truly add value—by communicating specialized knowledge within their particular field. But merely transmitting knowledge is often no longer enough. Today, speakers have a responsibility to make their talks relevant to the needs of their audience. When you listen to a sermon or speech, you may ask yourself, "How can I apply what you said to help my career?" Getting your content or message to stick requires active audience engagement that causes your audience to take notice. As you conclude your talk, be conscious of your call to action and connect it to them in a meaningful way.

Jasmine Henry, a content-marketing practitioner at Inbound Marketing Agency said, "When you inspire, amuse, or simply connect with your audience, the results can be just the boost your brand needs."[11] That's my charge to contemporary communicators. Don't be so concerned about the content. Focus also on connecting.

---

11   Jasmine Henry, "Branding for Small Business: Lessons from Big Business," *SocialMediaToday*
(July 2, 2013): http://www.socialmediatoday.com/users/jasminehenry.

Instead of blindly following conventions, think about what you're actually trying to accomplish when giving a speech, and ask yourself, "What is my goal? What will be different after communication has taken place?

REMOVE THE OBSTRUCTIONS: FORGING BONDS AND NEW CONNECTIONS

As the cognitive neuroscientist Matthew Lieberman pointed out in his book *Social*, our need to connect with others is as basic as our need for food and water.

While many experts proclaim that individuals are driven by self-interest, Lieberman implies that we suffer a great deal when our social bonds are threatened or severed. He asserts that the existence of social pain is a sign that evolution has made social connections a necessity not a luxury.

Think about the mottos of countless organizations, which say things like, "We aim to please," "We're here for you," or "Exceptional personal service is our only goal." What does this suggest to you about how people should converse or deliver presentations?

A speaker's primary goal is to connect with others. Begin with that goal in mind, and you'll find that everything else flows organically from there.

Why then do many speakers create barriers between themselves and their audience? Podiums. Lecterns. Tables. Any time you deliver a speech while standing behind an obstruction, you're reducing the chances of making a connection before you even begin.

Hiding behind a lectern means the audience can barely see you. The less they can see you, the less they can judge your body language and hence measure your credibility. Also the harder it is to see you, the less inclined they are to listen. We listen better when we see where sounds originate.

If possible, arrange to stand center stage with your body fully exposed to the audience. Although you might feel uncomfortable, you will look more open, vulnerable, and surprisingly more powerful.

THE POWER OF TED: REMOVE THE DISTANCE IN THE MODERN WORLD

With the advent of video and live teleconferences, how can you thrive in the modern world of mass communication? Where can you look to for models that inspire and encourage audience engagement?

That's easy. Go to the web and type in two words—TED Talk—and you'll find dozens of examples of effective audience engagement that avoid the need for lecterns or podiums. Every seventeen seconds, someone, somewhere in the world, is watching a TED (Technology, Entertainment, Design) Talk. If you have access to the Internet, it's likely you've either heard of or watched one.

Filmed at TED conferences and independent TEDx events, "their goal is to share Ideas Worth Spreading—in fields like science, technology, business, culture, art, and design—around the world in eighteen minutes or less."[12]

TED Talks are slick, well produced, and use particular lighting and on-stage visuals to effectively engage listeners. Taped in front of a live audience, they seek to enhance the relevance of the subject matter by making the audience feel as important as the speaker.

Copyright: Brad Horn, SoSUTV

Started in 2006 as an experiment with Internet video, TEDx presentations began with just six talks. TEDx producers didn't know at the time if people would sit for eighteen minutes to watch lectures online. By their own admission, producers didn't know their talks would take off in the next few years to such extraordinary heights.

Fast-forward to today, and TEDx Talks have surpassed over one billion views.[13] Not bad for an experiment!

---

12 http://www.ted.com/about/programs-initiatives/ted-talks

13 http://blog.ted.com/ted-reaches-its-billionth-video-view/

What can be concluded from their tremendous success? People have an enormous appetite to learn. TED's success underscores just how critical good timing, delivery, and clear communication techniques are to ensure proper audience engagement.

To watch a good TED Talk is to feel inspired. Given a speaker has eighteen minutes or less on stage, there is little room for wasted words. Even if you are watching on YouTube, there is something about their approach that makes you feel as if you are there. No distance, just connection!

TED is so much bigger than the usual high-energy presentations from self-proclaimed experts who want to sell you something. TED doesn't make you feel like you should reach for your credit card and BUY NOW. However, there is no question that they seek to inspire, persuade, and provoke change.

Most TED speakers are subject matter experts with something fresh, and often provocative, to deliver. They typically appear contrary to what we are accustomed to seeing in church, class, or business meetings. As the presenters stand on stage with an enormous screen behind them, what do you notice?

- They are hands free.

- With a microphone attached, their entire body is on view, since there is no lectern or other barrier to inhibit their delivery.

- They are in motion. They seem so natural and often look right into the eyes of the audience to ensure they build rapport and connect.

As even the best marketing minds know, gaining the attention of an audience for even thirty seconds is a tall order. Through the formula of keeping things short, lively, and entertaining, TED producers figured out how to make viewers feel like they are part of the event.

In the fall of 2015, I coached a senior at the University of Texas at Austin named William Dodd. On October 2nd in Reno, Nevada, he delivered a TEDx talk on his Rhetoric and Writing honors thesis called "The Pitfalls of 'Transparency': How Broadcasting Hinders Senate Deliberations." He relied on the Ten Commandments of Communicators and packed a wallop! No podium, no hand-held microphone, no place to hide. Just William: his body, voice, and heart! He delivered a powerful and compelling call to action in the modern world of leadership communication.

TED Talks draw you in, tell exceptional stories, and make you feel like you are important—with minimal distance, color, and energy to spare. The goal is to inspire, persuade, and provoke change in eighteen minutes, and pass it on to others.

Sound like leadership communication? Absolutely.

My Top Five Picks for the Most Effective TED Talks

1. **Ken Robinson: "Do Schools Kill Creativity?"**
   Robinson asserts that people and organizations acknowledge the current educational system is failing to

meet the challenges we face and is working zealously to create alternatives. His impassioned message underscores the need to better foster our natural-born capacities for creativity. Rethinking the approaches to the educational system is a strong start. His talk is gripping, authentic, and powerful.

2. **Amy Cuddy: "Your Body Language Shapes Who You Are."** Social psychologist Amy Cuddy discusses that body language affects how others see us but may also change how we see ourselves. This absorbing talk on nonverbal communication is thought provoking and a call to action on the need for self-awareness as a path to personal and professional growth.

3. **Stacy Kramer: "The Best Gift I Ever Survived."** This is a moving three-minute-and-seventeen-second story of how a frightening and traumatic experience can turn out to be a priceless gift. It's delivered with conviction, suspense, and power. Sometimes less is more.

4. **Brené Brown: "The Power of Vulnerability."** This is funny, poignant, and a lesson on human connection. Brown shares insights from her research on empathy and the importance of embracing our vulnerability. I love her positive attitude and loving spirit.

5. **Dan Ariely: "Are We in Control of Our Own Decisions?"** Behavioral economist Ariely boldly shares his research findings that humans are not as rational as you may think. It's great to listen to a credible expert challenge conventional wisdom to help us make better decisions.

CHAPTER 6

The Rule of Three: It's a Magic Number

In any extreme situation, you cannot survive for more than three minutes without air, three hours without shelter, three days without water.

—www.ruleof3survival.com

There was treason. Treachery. Civil unrest. It was nothing less than a clash between the defenders of an established order and a mob of revolutionaries intent on creating a new kind of society. King George III of England made it known that his colonial subjects were to follow the rule of law. Taxation without representation, decried the rebels, was abject tyranny. Reconciliation was no longer a viable course of action. Rebellion was their only option. Let the American Revolution begin!

On June 7, 1776, in Philadelphia, Pennsylvania, Richard Henry Lee of Virginia read a resolution before the Continental Congress that stated, "Resolved, that these United Colonies are, and of right ought to be, free and independent States. That they are absolved from all allegiance to the British Crown, and that all political connection between them and the State of Great Britain is, and ought to be, totally dissolved."

What followed was a document that remains one of the most important in the history of the world. Signed by fifty-six men from all thirteen colonies, the Declaration of Independence was—and remains to this day—one of the most elegantly written statements of individual rights ever put to paper. At the time it was written, it represented more than just the birth of a new country. It declared a set of core values that fostered discussions of liberty throughout much of the world.

Note the way Thomas Jefferson, the author of the declaration, distilled the concepts of the revolution into three core ideas: life, liberty, and the pursuit of happiness.

"We hold these truths to be self-evident, that all men are created equal, that they are endowed by their Creator with certain unalienable Rights, that among these are life, liberty, and the pursuit of happiness." That phrase—"life, liberty, and the pursuit of happiness"—remains timeless in large part because it's so simple. It's as poetic as it is impactful. It was so influential, in fact, that it inspired the French people to pursue their own freedom and adopt the nationalistic slogan: "liberty, equality, fraternity."

Both phrases draw on a classical rhetorical technique, developed centuries ago by the ancient Greeks, which said that words or phrases delivered in threes are inherently easy to remember. Jefferson and the

French used a hendiatris, a figure of speech where three successive words are used to express a single central idea. Used as a slogan or motto, this is known as a tripartite motto. Countless examples are seen in the American government and branches of American armed services that include:

- **"Duty, Honor, Country."** This is from the US Military Academy's coat of arms and is a striking expression of their ideals.

- **"The Few, The Proud, the Marines."** This is from the US Marine Corps' advertising slogan.

- **"Fly-Fight-Win."** The US Air Force, which formerly used "Aim High" as their motto, augmented it with the Rule of Three in 2010. It's now a "two-part expression, a call to action with a response to commitment."

The Rule of Three can also refer to a collection of words, phrases, or sentences. A triad, for example, is a group or set of three connected people or things. "The Clintons united for the final debate with Bill, Hillary, and Chelsea appearing together on stage." The technique is often used in oral storytelling, films, and advertising. We read or saw films about the Three Musketeers, the Three Little Pigs, and the Three Amigos.

A tricolon is a specific application of the Rule of Three, in which three words or phrases are equal in length and grammatical form. Some well-known examples include:

- "Tell me and I forget. Teach me and I may remember. Involve me and I will learn." —Benjamin Franklin

- "We cannot dedicate, we cannot consecrate, we cannot hallow this ground." —Abraham Lincoln from the Gettysburg Address

- "If there is anyone out there who still doubts that America is a place where all things are possible; who still wonders if the dream of our founders is alive in our time; who still questions the power of our democracy, tonight is your answer." —President Barack Obama.

An advertising pioneer in the 1950s named E. St. Elmo-Lewis articulated three key copywriting principles, which he felt were crucial for effective advertising:

1. The mission of an advertisement is to attract a reader so he will look at the advertisement and start to read it;

2. Then to interest him, so that he will continue to read it;

3. Then to convince him, so that when he has read it he will believe it.

He felt if an advertisement contained these three qualities, it would be successful.

For speakers, three is—and always has been—the perfect number. List two things— black and white, up and down, right and wrong—and audiences tend to contrast the two. Rattle off a string of four ideas and people often forget half of what was said.

There's a certain rhythm, however, to linking together three ideas that resonates with listeners and readers. We're accustomed, for instance, to using the Rule of Three to elicit action. Think about the movie business: *lights, camera, action.* Or a high-school track meet:

ready, set, go. Or when you're teaching children how to safely cross a street: *stop, look, listen.*

Throughout history, great speakers have long used the Rule of Three for maximum impact. Think about President John F. Kennedy. As mentioned previously, in his quest to win the space race, JFK employed the Rule of Three to ensure that his messages stuck in the minds of his audience: "The challenge is one that we are willing to accept, one we are unwilling to postpone, and one which we intend to win."

Whenever you sit down to write a speech, keep the idea of the Rule of Three central in your mind. Not only is it an effective means of distilling lots of information into digestible pieces, but it will make your message more memorable as well.

We use the Rule of Three everywhere. A few additional examples include:

- **Father, Son, Holy Spirit:** Christian doctrine of God in three persons

- **Earth, Wind, & Fire:** iconic 1970s American rock band

- **Snap, Crackle, Pop:** Rice Krispies cereal mascots created in 1930 and still used to sell you breakfast to this very day

When you stand and deliver, be conscious of creating a sense of order that is clear, concise, and compelling. Whether it's the past, present, or future, make your speeches effective, powerful, and memorable. And keep in mind that one of the paths to being a great public speaker is to practice, practice, practice.

CASE STUDY: SHERYL SANDBERG SPARKS A REVOLUTION WITH THE RULE OF THREE

On Tuesday, May 17, 2011, on the campus of Barnard College, Facebook COO Sheryl Sandberg opened her commencement speech with the following lead:

You may not remember one word I say. You may not remember who your graduation speaker is (although for the record, Sheryl with an S). You may not even remember that it was raining and we had to move inside.

But you will remember what matters, which is how you feel as you sit here, as you walk across the stage, as you start the next phase of your life.

Note Sandberg's immaculate use of the Rule of Three here. She has utilized the Primacy Effect, and her skillful use of repetition immediately builds rapport with her audience. By saying "you" to open each phrase, she is speaking directly to each member of the audience. I recommend that all of my clients watch—or at least read the transcript of—Sandberg's speech on Barnard's website, as it offers a good example of a blueprint to successfully use the Rule of Three in different ways throughout a speech.

It relies on a solid structure, relevant statistics, and stories to support her content. She opens and closes it with impact, while addressing the main problem within forty-five seconds and using the Rule of Three to introduce her key points and calls to action. It's not surprising that the speech went viral almost immediately after it was presented, later inspiring Sandberg to write her international bestseller, *Lean In: Women, Work, and the Will to Lead*, which also uses the Rule of Three for dramatic effect.

Pay close attention to Sandberg's speech, and you'll notice just how often she relies on the Rule of Three to underscore important moments and keep her talk moving along at a brisk pace.

Early on she uses the Rule of Three to mark the significance of her audience's great milestone. "Today is a day of celebration. Today is a day of thanks. Today is a day of reflection."

As a follow-up, she quickly shifts the focus by asking each graduate to reflect on today's significance. To get the audience thinking about her topic, she asks three questions: "What will you do with this education you worked so hard to achieve? What in the world needs to change? What part do you plan on playing in changing it?"

Consider the oblique way that Sandberg answers her own questions, chiefly by referencing a book by Pulitzer Prize winners Nicholas Kristof and Sheryl WuDunn called *Half the Sky*. She is subtly using historical context to guide her audience to answer those questions in a particular way.

Drawing from *Half the Sky*, Sandberg argues that the fundamental moral challenge for the nineteenth century was slavery; the twentieth century's was totalitarianism; and for our century, the oppression of girls and women around the world—another savvy use of the Rule of Three.

In the midst of this address to Barnard's students, she even used the Rule of Three to remind everyone of her employer's mission:

"Connect the whole world. Make the world more open. More transparent."

Think about what Sandberg is doing. She's going back in time in order to pull her audience through to the present day. Then she hits the audience with a powerful statement: "As we sit here looking at this magnificent blue-robed class," says Sandberg, "we have to admit something that's sad but true: men run the world."

Notice in the video how Sandberg lets that statement hang in the air for a second for dramatic effect. Then she delivers a trio of shocking stats:

- Of 190 heads of state, nine are women.

- Of all the parliaments around the world, women hold thirteen percent of those seats.

- Of corporate America top jobs, fifteen percent are held by women—numbers which have not moved at all in the past nine years.

Sandberg planted a seed in the minds of her primarily female audience by addressing them directly. Notice, then, how the pattern of three continues with equal force, "So today, we turn to you. You are the promise for a more equal world. You are our hope. We need women at all levels, including the top, to change the dynamic, reshape the conversation, make sure women's voices are heard."

Her close is an impassioned plea of hope and action. "I hope you find true meaning, contentment, passion."

She then lets the audience consider the weight of her message by encouraging them to "Go home tonight and ask yourselves, 'What would I do if I weren't afraid?' And then go do it!" Sandberg's close is a classic call to action. Go do it. And sure enough, after Sandberg's speech made the rounds and her book found its way into bookstores, people transformed her ideas into nothing less than a movement.

Sandberg's speech—and the book it inspired—is a call to action to change the conversation from what women can't do to what they can. It has also become a rallying cry for men and women to work together to achieve gender equality worldwide—a movement that started, appropriately enough, with a speech that sparked a revolution. She rebooted feminism, inspired a generation to act, and provoked women around the world to lean in.

CHAPTER 7

Speakers Must Punctuate: Punctuation from Passion

The August 23, 2015, headline of *The New York Times* read:

A Plunge in China Rattles
Markets across the Globe

Stocks around the world tumbled in volatile trading on Monday, leaving investors to wonder how much government officials can and will do to insulate the global economy from the turmoil. The upheaval in the markets began with another rout in China that drew comparisons to the 1987 crash in the United States known as "Black Monday.

The large-type front-page headline, like the one above, became popular in the late nineteenth century when increased competition between newspapers led to the proliferation of bold, attention-grabbing headlines. Readers were immediately drawn to the words, and soon newspapers employed all manner of typographical embellishments to grab people's attention, including **bold** type, <u>underlined</u> phrases, and *italicized* words.

Even to this day, whenever a truly momentous event occurs, newspapers will use typographical embellishments to help make their papers stand out on a newsstand. On September 12, 2001, *The New York Times* headline read **"U.S. ATTACKED"** in huge bold letters. In slightly smaller letters—yet in bigger than normal type—the sub headline read, "HIJACKED JETS DESTROY TWIN TOWERS AND HIT PENTAGON IN DAY OF TERROR."

Mere words? Hardly. Newspapers skillfully arrange sequences of words in ways that make us feel the full impact of important stories. Sometimes it's horror, contempt, and anger: **"GERMANY AND ITALY DECLARE WAR ON U.S."** Other times, it's pure inspiration: **"THE CROWNING GLORY. EVEREST IS CLIMBED!"** Although each of these news stories may contain hundreds of words, it's these eye-catching flourishes that tend to make the most lasting impressions.

The very same principles apply to speech communication. During a presentation, it's difficult for listeners to absorb everything a speaker says, especially when a series of ideas is coming at them in rapid-fire succession. Thus I encourage my clients to highlight key feelings, attitudes, and words by emphasizing certain phrases more boldly than others.

You should always ask yourself these two questions when giving a speech:

1. What do we want the audience to think, feel, or do to move them closer to our cause?

2. What is different after communication has taken place?

Highlighting every single word you say is counterproductive to those goals. Be selective. Consider which concepts and phrases deserve more attention than others. When we speak, there are a variety of techniques that will make our meaning clear, such as emphasis, intonation, rhythm, and strategic pauses.

When we're writing, we use punctuation marks and typographic elements—like commas, italics, bold letters, exclamation points, and question marks—to represent those rhythms on the page. It's a consistent and sensible system. Every punctuation mark has one or more particular functions, and we learn when and where to place those punctuation marks as we learn how to write.

Many speakers, however, forget to punctuate their sentences when they are delivering a speech. Speaking in a flat style may bore, frustrate, or (worst of all) confuse your audience. They will disengage and stop paying attention if they don't perceive that you are enthusiastic about your topic.

While some people speak with an unvaried cadence when they get nervous, others simply find it too challenging to vary their delivery. Others aren't conscience of the need to vary and do what feels natural to them. Don't fall into these traps. Start by being self-aware of how to improve this aspect of speech communication.

However, speaking with too much energy and enthusiasm can work against you. I've witnessed countless speakers rush through their talks at lightning speed, failing to punctuate their sentences in the ways that they would if they were writing them down. Ultimately, they leave their audiences feeling confused and bewildered.

For instance, an English professor once wrote on the chalkboard, "A woman without her man is nothing." He then asked students to punctuate it. The males in the class wrote: "A woman, without her man, is nothing." The females in the class wrote, "A woman: without her, man is nothing." Seven words whose meaning radically changes due to the power of punctuation.

Try this simple sentence: "Let's eat Grandma." If you deliver that sentence quickly, giving equal weight to each of those three words, you are saying that, at the dinner table, grandma will be the main entrée.

However, if you punctuate that sentence as "Let's eat, Grandma," you're actually offering your grandmother a call to action. You're saying to Grandma, "Let's go to the dinner table and eat." Commas change meanings, and in this case, can save a life!

> # Let's eat Grandma
>
> ### or
>
> # Let's eat, Grandma.
>
> ---
>
> **Punctuation: It Saves Lives**

Listen to a speech with improper emphasis and you'll likely describe the experience as negative. Emphasis is crucial and must be mastered. When everything or nothing is emphasized, how do you know what's important? If you're passionate about the subject matter, the audience will think it's important too. Punctuation makes that possible. At the end of the day, passion and punctuation should be viewed as opposite sides of the same coin.

Since the listener doesn't have the luxury of reading your words, it's your responsibility to *properly punctuate*! Next time you find yourself rushing through a speech, ask yourself if you want to eat grandma or eat with grandma? Intent is not enough. It's how an audience receives your words that matters most. As a wise friend once told me, "We want people to judge us by our intentions, but they actually judge us by our actions and our words."

PASSION PRECEDES PUNCTUATION: AN EDIE MAGNUS CASE STUDY

If you want to get a free education on how to properly punctuate your speech while telling a compelling story, I recommend watching a skilled broadcaster deliver the nightly news.

According to Edie Magnus, a thirty-year TV news veteran who has served as an anchor for three major networks, one of the key tricks of the anchor trade is to treat words with proper emphasis, force, and feeling. Good anchors, in other words, punctuate their speech.

Since the audience can't see commas, question marks, or exclamation points, express them in ways that make them care. Be sincere and passionate. Stories and speeches must come from within and make their way to an audience with power and conviction. As Magnus so eloquently told me, "It's passion that drives punctuation."

For the nationally televised documentary *Cry for Help*, Magnus had the following narration: "Across the country, dozens of teenagers kill themselves." Then she paused, before saying slowly, "Twenty-eight a week. That's a rate of four per day." She's not just punctuating for the sake of punctuating. She wants people to feel the effects of the stories she's presenting.

Think of proper speech punctuation as applying force to the important words and subordinating the unimportant. By doing this effectively, you're not just speaking. You're telling a story in an interpretive way.

"I pause to emphasize things based on what I genuinely, authentically believe to be important about the story and why I'm telling it," says Magnus. Everything is in the service of why. One speaker will offer one interpretation of the story. Another will emphasize other elements to arrive at a different conclusion. "Punctuation," she insists, "is not a paint-by-numbers thing."

According to Magnus, the integration of speaking with punctuation and getting your audience to care has three key considerations:

1. You are never just disseminating information.

2. You tell a story you care about, which in turn drives how you tell it.

3. You use punctuation to drive the meaning you want to convey.

In other words, great communicators speak with intent.

STRIKE WITH FORCE: FINDING THE RIGHT SYLLABLE

When giving a presentation, you can punctuate your speech in a variety of ways, including with physical gestures. You can raise your eyebrows. Furrow your brow. Take a moment to smile. All these physical movements can help you draw your audience's attention to a particular element of your speech.

For instance, if you say, "Our sales are up fifteen percent!" try supporting that impressive statistic with an index finger pointing straight up to the heavens. I once saw a speaker relay positive news while pointing in the wrong direction, down instead of up. This mismatch between his words and body language caused the audience to doubt the sincerity of his claim.

Body language misaligned with words generates suspicion and mistrust. And once trust begins to erode, people stop *listening*.

Often skilled communicators emphasize a particular part or sound of a word in order to express a feeling or to highlight an idea.

- The first syllable of a key word is pronounced louder than other syllables: FAN-tastic.

- A key word is spoken more slowly: *Pleeeease*, go home and get some rest.

- A vowel sound is stretched: "O O O O O U T . . . standing!"

If you want to deliver an impactful speech, don't emphasize each syllable with the same force. Try not to hit an unimportant syllable with too much emphasis and then rush over the important ones.

Take this sentence, for example: "There is no failure, only feedback." Which words do you emphasize? Try this in different combinations to see which sticks: "There is *no* failure, *only* feedback." Or, "There is no *failure*, only *feedback*." Speak it aloud. You may want to emphasize *feedback*, as that is the principal idea of your declaration. Or are you emphasizing *no such thing as failure*?

As you learned in chapter 1 with the Primacy/Recency Effect, think carefully about what information you want to leave the listener with. *No failure* or . . . *only feedback*?

Two words in opposition can make the phrase more memorable. Contrast and comparison are matters of emphasis and a device to highlight your message.

Here's a perfect example. Read this sentence as if you were reading a newspaper headline: "**THE RED SOX WIN THE WORLD SERIES**. Can you believe it?"

Now try to read that same sentence without the change in cadence. "**THE RED SOX WIN THE WORLD SERIES, CAN YOU BELIEVE IT?**" Or "The Red Sox win the world series. Can you believe it?"

Which approach is the most effective? An attempt to emphasize everything yields no emphasis at all. Great speakers make key words stand out like mountain peaks. They read their "bolded letters" with intensity or a sense of wonder.

Take, for example, this memorable speech by Al Pacino in the film *Any Given Sunday*:

> On this team, we *fight* for that inch. On this team, we *tear* ourselves and everyone around us to pieces for that inch. We *claw* with our fingernails for that inch. 'Cause we know when we add up all those inches that's going to

make the f…ing difference between *winning* and *losing*, between *living* and *dying*.

Notice that the mountain peaks immediately catch our attention and create an emotional reaction. "Claw" conveys a feeling that supports the speech's title "Inch by Inch," while Pacino's winning/losing and living/dying constructions are great examples of the compare/contrast device.

Imagine Pacino's speech if the mountain-peak words were treated like all the others. "Claw" would be hidden in plain sight; it wouldn't emphasize the inch-by-inch feeling the coach is trying to steer into the minds of his players. By comparing winning and losing to living and dying, he uses a metaphor to stress the importance of the upcoming game. Metaphors help highlight the message of an address in ways that direct language often cannot.

To emphasize a word or words, say them differently than the words surrounding them. If you have been speaking loudly, use a whisper to intensify the emotion. If you have been going fast, move slower when you come to a more emphatic word.

Using language as a tool goes way beyond grammar and vocabulary. In order to persuade your audience, it's essential you integrate emphasis and rhythm. While giving stress to words highlights certain sounds, rhythm is the musicality of ups and downs that give a sentence a smooth tempo.

Sometimes, for even greater emphasis, try stressing every syllable in a single word. For instance, "I *com-pleeete-ly* understand how you feel." You can also stretch out each word in a sentence for extra-special emphasis. "*Give—me—liberty—or—give—me—death.*"

There are no hard-and-fast rules on how and when you choose to punctuate. Like a good newspaper editor, you decide what should stick. If you are giving the same speech twice, try different combinations of oral punctuation to see what works best.

Do everything you can to transform your presentation from ordinary to unforgettable. Under the right conditions, you and your audience can feed off of each other's passion and excitement. Trust your intuition and experience to be your guide. When you do, you'll inspire, persuade, and provoke change in ways that may surprise you!

It starts when the *speaker* punctuates!

CHAPTER 8

The Power of the Pause: Impact from Surprising Places

"The right word may be effective,
but no word was ever as effective
as a rightly timed pause."

—Mark Twain[14]

I see a whole army of my countrymen [pause]

here in defiance of tyranny. [pause]

You've come to fight as free men [pause]

---

14 Autobiographical dictation, 11 October 1907. Published in *Autobiography of Mark Twain, Vol. 3* (University of California Press, 2015).

and free men you are. [pause]

What will you do with that freedom? [pause]]

Will you fight? [pause]

Fight and you may die. [pause]

Run, and you'll live [pause] . . . at least a while. [pause]

And dying in your beds, many years from now . . . [pause]

would you be willin' to trade ALL the days, from this day to that, for one chance, [pause]

just one chance, [pause]

to come back here and tell our enemies that they may take our lives, [long pause]

but they'll never take OUR FREEDOM!

—William Wallace, *Braveheart*

I n 1296, King Edward I of England took advantage of a succession crisis in Scotland and imposed himself as the ruler of Britain. Within months, Scottish unrest hurled the country into chaos. William Wallace, played by Mel Gibson in the movie *Braveheart*, led his outnumbered Scottish soldiers into battle to defeat an English regiment at the Battle of Stirling Bridge.

In the film, Wallace addresses his troops just before a critical siege with the above words—which still give me chills twenty years after the movie premiered. What is it about Wallace's call to action that is so powerful, compelling, and memorable?

For starters, he learned to punctuate. Perhaps he read chapter 7 of this book. Given how that's unlikely, notice how Wallace rallies his troops by using the right words . . . in the right order . . . with just the right inflections.

Like Wallace, imbue your speech with emotion, force, and meaning. Through the use of dramatic effect, your words can convey an explosive intensity that strikes deep into the hearts and minds of your listeners.

Great speakers in every field and occupation rely on the power of well-timed pauses to grab their audience's attention. During presidential debates, it's often the candidates who control the pause and the pace of their deliveries who command the stage, compelling us to listen more intently to their words, tone, and delivery.

When speakers are rushed or flustered, they seem out of control, quickly diminishing their credibility. Once we disengage from that candidate, it's not likely we'll listen to anything more. We'll wait for the superior speaker to take over and follow him or her to victory.

Take, for example, the 1980 presidential debate between incumbent President Jimmy Carter and Ronald Reagan, the former governor of California. When people watched both candidates speak, there was something distinctive about Reagan's delivery. Whatever your political affiliation, he spoke in a way that was compelling and commanding. You didn't just hear his words; you could feel the emotion and humor behind his words. Trained as an actor, he exploited the speaking skills he cultivated on screen and brought them to the presidential stage.

During the 1984 presidential debates, when many wondered if he was too old to be president at age seventy-three, he said to his opponent, Walter Mondale: "I will not make age an issue of this campaign. [pause] I am not going to exploit for political purposes, [pause] my opponent's youth and inexperience."

In electing Mr. Reagan, there was little doubt he would be a good communicator. What surprised many people is that he continued to develop his oratory skills while in office, earning the title "The Great Communicator."

THE POWER OF THE PAUSE: TIPS & TECHNIQUES

"Mr. Gorbachev . . . [pause for dramatic effect] . . . tear down this wall."

Say the above phrase aloud, making sure to stick that pause. Now repeat the phrase without a pause. Do you hear the difference?

With my clients, I try not only to help them develop useful techniques but also to explain why they can be effective in practice. In terms of pause power, there are three primary reasons why strategically placed moments of silence are essential for all speakers to add to their repertoire.

1. **Pauses allow the speaker to concentrate their energies on a call to action.** Pauses provide listeners with the opportunity to reflect on what has come before and what they expect will follow. They are designed to call attention

to themselves—to stand out and help listeners realize that something important is about to be said.

In *The Pursuit of Happyness*, Will Smith plays the real-life Chris Gardner, a homeless single father struggling to raise his young son and succeed as a newly minted stockbroker. In spite of financial hardships, Gardner never stops believing in himself and transfers that faith to the youngster. In one of the film's many poignant moments, he uses pause power to emphasize that dreams can come true. It's the silence between the words that creates the biggest impact.

"Don't ever let somebody tell you [pause] you can't do something. All right? You got a dream [pause]. You gotta protect it. People can't do somethin' themselves, they wanna tell you you can't do it. If you want somethin', go get it. Period."

2. **They create suspense.** Great movies, especially espionage thrillers, know how to keep an audience engaged. You learn a lot about dialogue and delivery that can be transferred into speech mode. Take *Bridge of Spies*, Steven Spielberg's well-crafted treasure starring Tom Hanks. Hanks plays the real-life James B. Donovan, a lawyer who defended a British defector to the Soviet Union accused of spying during the Cold War. Watch the movie intently, and you'll notice how well the scenes build tension through conversation. Hear the words, and listen carefully to the silence that amplifies the drama. As with any captivating story, we're anxious to hear what's coming as we anticipate the next line. In one scene, a government agent named Williams explains to

his colleagues the gravity of the situation with the Soviet Union. In his attempt to persuade, he pauses for intensity and dramatic effect.

"We are engaged in a war. [pause] This war does not for the moment involve men at arms [pause]; it involves information. You will be collecting information. You will be gathering intelligence about the enemy [pause]. The intelligence you gather could give us the upper hand in a full thermonuclear exchange with the Soviet Union, [pause] or it could prevent one."

It's unlikely you'll be called on to deliver a speech on the fate of American freedom. Use pause techniques however to strengthen your delivery and cause the audience to pay closer attention to words or ideas you seek to magnify. As Alan Alda says about acting and the power of the pause, "It's the stuff between the lines that makes it a great performance."

3.   **They control the overall pace of delivery.** The audience has cognitive limitations and can only absorb a certain amount of information at one time. Pausing slows down your rate of delivery to match the listening capacity of the audience. It buys time to engage the audience and lets them absorb the words you have emphasized. To use a volleyball metaphor, a pause is the set up to the spike. Take a famous example from Star Wars: "No. [pause] I am your father."

My advice: Take your time. You have more of it than you think. Audiences will be patient if you have something that's thought provoking and memorable to say. They know that a good line or idea is worth the wait.

Following are some "power of the pause" techniques to practice as you rehearse your speeches:

- **Clause Pause:** Use short pauses where there is normally a comma that separates two clauses or particular items in a long list. "Wanting to impress my girlfriend [pause] I brought flowers, [pause] wine, [pause] and dessert."

- **Sentence Pause:** Use medium pauses wherever a period, question mark, or exclamation point normally appears in order to separate two sentences. "After six days of climbing, we summited Mount Kilimanjaro. [pause] I can't believe I actually did it!"

- **Paragraph Pause:** Use long pauses when you transition from one idea to the next. In written language, we always indent when starting a new paragraph. The same is true with speaking. The pause sends a signal preparing the listener that something important or unique is about to happen. President Barack Obama, in a 2009 speech to sell his plan for the Affordable Care Act, said, "Since health care represents one-sixth of our economy, I believe it makes more sense to build on what works and fix what doesn't, rather than try to build an entirely new system from scratch." Instead of leaping straight into the details, he took a very long pause and incorporated the Rule of Three, so his audience could grasp both the concept and the details of his plan: "The plan I'm announcing tonight would meet three basic goals. It will provide more security and stability to those who have health insurance. It will provide insurance for those who don't. And it will slow the growth of healthcare costs for our families, our businesses, and our government."

- **Emphasis Pause:** While creating emphasis is a result of using strategic pauses, sometimes you may want to draw attention to one or two key words. Pause immediately before and after that word or phrase, thus signaling the listener that what you are about to say is important. *[pause] And the Oscar goes to [pause] Tom Hanks!*

- **Rhetorical Question Pause:** It's gratifying to watch heads nod in an audience when you pose a rhetorical question. This motivates your audience to stay engaged as they contemplate the answer to your question. Because most people recognize a rhetorical question when they hear it, they seem certain you won't call on them to offer a response and thus maintain their attention on your words.

  Overall, your aim is to provoke a thought that lends credence to your message. "Please think for a moment [pause] what would life be like [pause] if we could only love [pause] but never hate?" On the other hand, failure to pause after posing a rhetorical question often frustrates your audience. They've been asked to contemplate something, and you've moved on without giving them time to think about it. Rhetorical questions help you quickly gauge who is paying attention and who is not by their body language. If you see wandering eyes and minimal head nods, it's a wake-up call to make adjustments to your approach.

- **Power Pause:** I often open my speeches this way. Before I utter a word, I lock my eyes onto my audience. Each second I wait serves two purposes: It allows me to center myself as I silently assess the dynamic of the room. Second, it strengthens the impact of my opening words. This has to be done with tremendous confidence, lest the silence seems forced and awkward. Think about a rocket launch: *three . . . two . . . one . . . speak!*

Opening with a pause can be a valuable asset to speakers. How often have you seen a speaker stand up and immediately launch into his speech? One word follows another; the listener has a hard time separating what should be stressed and what should not. No one remembers the opening, because it doesn't stand out.

Think about President Lincoln and how he might have delivered the Gettysburg Address:

- Movement 1: Lincoln looks out over the crowd.
- Movement 2: He pauses for a powerful launch as the audience waits in anticipation.
- Movement 3: He says, "Four score and seven years ago, our fathers brought forth on this continent, a new nation."

Imagine that scene, and feel the confluence of power and eloquence in one complete package.

- **Punch Line:** We can learn a great deal from comedians in speech communication. Their livelihoods depend on perfect timing. When telling jokes, which are often stories, their objective is to create a heightened sense of anticipation. They are signaling to the audience that (wait for it) a payoff is about to come.

  They pause immediately before a punch line to create tension—and then immediately after to allow the audience to release their laughter. Remember to extend the pause for as long as there is laughter. Otherwise, your words will compete for attention and your effectiveness will be diminished.

Watch the great comedians (I'm partial to Seinfeld), and notice their approach. "These pretzels [pause] are making me thirsty!" Even if you don't intend to be funny, spontaneous laughter often presents itself at the most unexpected times. When that happens, look to your favorite comedian to be your guide.

Resist the impulse to speak over the applause. Allow time to reset. While it's not likely you have a stand-up routine, the tactics for comedy and speech delivery are equally effective in a boardroom as in a comedy club.

- **Glass of Water Pause / Let Me Think about This Pause:** When giving longer presentations, you're prone to getting thirsty. I've seen speakers avoid taking time to drink some water, only to diminish their ability to close a speech with power because they were parched. Many people I coach are hesitant to do this, as they worry it looks unnatural. That's not the case. Audiences are so accustomed to the sight of speakers drinking water that they often don't even notice. The glass of water pause is an effective tactic that should be used more often. While you're taking a sip, use that time to gather your thoughts, refresh, and continue where you left off.

- **Check My Notes:** I often take audience questions that require time for me to contemplate and fully answer. The last thing you want is to offer an audience a knee-jerk reaction to an important question. In their quest to please and look responsive, many presenters blurt out half-formed answers at lighting speed, only to regret it later.

Consider what Barbara Bush said on whether her son Jeb should run for president: "There are other people out there that are very qualified, and we've had enough Bushes."

Who could remember what else she might have said after hearing that line? All the other words she said during that interview are forgotten.

Think about the implications of that statement. If Bush's mom doesn't think he should run (for whatever reason), why should anyone else think so? The lesson: take time to contemplate your answers before you respond.

One effective way to buy time to a tough question is to say, "I have a reference to your question in my notes. Give me a second to check so that I get it right." While you may not be checking anything at all in your notes, buying extra time can mean the difference between persuasion and destruction. It gives the listener time to catch up too; so it's a win/win. They won't remember the pause. They will, however, commit to memory your response.

HOW TO CREATE A POETIC SILENCE

How long should you pause when inserting a moment of silence in your presentations?

There are no hard-and-fast rules. Pauses can last a fraction of a second to several seconds. The length of your pause depends on your tone, message, and style. Also factor in your audience, their patience, and level of engagement.

In general, however, it's best to vary the length of your pauses consistently throughout a speech. Don't get into a pattern where the listener can predict how long your pause will last. Experiment with varying lengths. Comma pauses for words tend to be briefer than sentence pauses, which are a bit shorter than your paragraph pauses.

I videotape many of my clients and, like a movie director, do several takes to see which one works best. It will seem awkward at first; most pauses do. However, once you master this technique, all other aspects of your delivery are bound to significantly improve.

Take care not to overwork the pause, lest you sound rehearsed and stilted. Some speakers deliver everything they say with a pause attached. It's as if each word they communicate could eradicate cancer or solve world hunger. Don't fall into that trap. Use them judiciously. Sometimes less is more.

Try this piece of "The Road Not Taken" by Robert Frost with pauses and without. Listen to the difference:

I shall be telling this with a sigh

Somewhere ages and ages hence:

Two roads diverged in a wood, and I—

I took the one less traveled by,

And that has made all the difference.

Pausing is perfectly natural. It's how we breathe. So take the time to integrate words, punctuations, and pauses as you communicate.

Many speakers are nervous, worried about how they will be perceived. They are also concerned they will be interrupted, only to throw off their own rhythm. Desperate to finish and get off stage, they rush through the speech as if they're running late to catch the last plane out of town. If you want to be understood and remembered, slow down. Take your time, pause where appropriate, and let your natural vocal rhythms take over.

The best leaders, the ones who communicate power, are calm, collected, and compelling. They speak with tremendous control, use pauses effectively, and convey confidence and conviction to their audience.

Remember the old maxim: Speak in such a way that others love to listen to you. Listen in such a way that others love to speak to you.

WHAT SPEECH COMMUNICATORS LEARN FROM MARK TWAIN ON THE POWER OF THE PAUSE

Let us make a special effort to stop communicating with each other, so we can have some conversation.

—Mark Twain

ep·i·gram *(noun):* a pithy saying or remark expressing an idea in a clever and amusing way

If Mark Twain were alive today, he would have more followers on Twitter than Oprah Winfrey. I enjoy reading his books and profit enormously from his speeches, quips, and quotes. His powerful phrases, almost always numbering less than 140 characters, are essential ingredients in my speech recipe book. While there are far too many quotes to point out a favorite, his thoughts on the essence of communication are priceless:

> *It is better to keep your mouth closed and let people think you are a fool than to open it and remove all doubt.*

Twain's epigrams not only make me laugh, but they are sound advice to anyone contemplating a career dependent on public speaking:

There are only two types of speakers in the world. The nervous and the liars.

What does Twain suggest to those who show no sign of nerves? Plenty, including the fact that audiences are predisposed to not believe a word they say.

In the *Autobiography of Mark Twain*, you can read many of his anecdotes, hilarious quotes, and fascinating details about his life. He was a great storyteller who overcame stage fright early in his career. (Proof that there is hope for all of us.) He managed to live through that frightful experience and go on to enthrall audiences for the next fifty years.

Although his writings remain classics in the canon of American literature, none of us has the luxury of actually hearing him speak. We do know, however, that he promoted his books through forceful, humorous, and compelling speeches. His speeches sold out everywhere he went and made his listeners laugh, cry, and, cheer—and his oratory skills were lavished with praise.

Bored audiences would rejoice when they heard Twain was next up to speak. His exaggerated drawl sent a spark into the crowd. William Dean Howells, in an introduction to the book *Mark Twain's Speeches*, said, "He was so consummate an actor that to hear him speak was twice as satisfactory as to read his fancies."

He brought his words to life in several ways. Here are the top ten lessons we can learn from Mark Twain:

1. **On storytelling** (encouraging to us mere mortals): "The humorous story is strictly a work of art—high and delicate art—and only an artist can tell it; but no art is necessary in telling the comic and the witty story; anybody can do it."

2. **On preparation:** "It usually takes me more than three weeks to prepare a good impromptu speech."

3. **On brevity:** "No one ever complained about a speech being too short."

4. **On stage fright:** "If there is an awful, horrible malady in the world, it is stage fright—and seasickness. They are a pair. I had stage fright then for the first and last time. I was only seasick once, too. It was on a little ship on which there were two hundred other passengers. I—was—sick. I was so sick that there wasn't any left for those other two hundred *passengers.*"

5. **On impact:** "Right in the middle of the speech I had placed a gem. I had put in a moving, pathetic part, which was to get at the hearts and souls of my hearers. When I delivered it, they did just what I hoped and expected. They sat silent and awed. I had touched them."

6. **On pauses:** "That impressive silence, that eloquent silence, that geometrically progressive silence which often achieves a desired effect where no combination of words howsoever felicitous could accomplish it . . . For one audience, the pause will be short; for another a little longer; for another a shade longer still; the performer must vary the length of the

pause to suit the shades of difference between audiences… I used to play with the pause as other children play with a toy."

7. **On words:** "The difference between the right word and the almost right word is the difference between lightning and a lightning bug."

8. **On school:** "I have never let my schooling interfere with my education."

9. **On honesty:** "If you tell the truth, you don't have to remember anything."

10. **On career climbing:** "The secret to getting ahead is getting started."

One more note on Twain. He organized his speeches into small pieces and used short sentences. In other words, he faithfully employed the Rule of Three, paying close attention to creating a beginning, middle, and end to each of his stories. He then approached his speeches using this disciplined template:

The Introduction:

- Acknowledge the audience.

- Say specifically—yet briefly—what you are talking about.

- Make them laugh.

The Middle

- Move it along.

- Leave things out. Do not explain everything.

- Use rhetorical devices. Examples include compare and contrast, self-deprecating humor, callbacks, similes, and metaphors.

The End

- Say it again in as few lines as you can.

- Say thanks.

- Make them laugh.

Learning the art and science of speech communication can be cruel, challenging, and exhilarating, all at the same time. It is why Jerry Seinfeld once artfully said, "According to most studies, people's number-one fear is public speaking. Death is number two."

Twain's greatest words of wisdom are a reminder to challenge yourself to be different. Your success comes not from fitting in but by standing out. Find your own voice—a distinctive style that sets you apart from everyone else. Learning to command the power of the pause is a great start!

"Whenever you find yourself on the side of the majority, it is time to pause and reflect."

—Mark Twain

CHAPTER 9

Animate the Visuals: What's Old Is What's New

"Visuals express ideas in a snackable manner."

—Kim Garst, CEO, Boom Social: Social Selling Made Simple[15]

Tony Robbins is an American motivational speaker, personal finance instructor, and self-help author. In a LinkedIn post in November of 2014, he published an article entitled "The 6 Human Needs: Why We Do What We Do." In the piece, he wrote, "While each human being is unique, we also share nervous systems that function in the same way. There are also six fundamental needs that everyone has in common, and all behavior is simply an attempt to meet those six needs."

---

15 Elena Lathrop, "15 Internal Communications Best Practices for 2015," https://enplug.com/blog/15-internal-communications-best-practices-for-2015.

According to Robbins, those six fundamental needs are:

1. **Certainty:** assurance you can avoid pain and gain pleasure

2. **Significance:** feeling unique, important, or special

3. **Connection/Love:** a strong feeling of closeness or union with someone or something

4. **Growth:** an expansion of capacity, capability, or understanding

5. **Contribution:** a sense of service and focus on helping, giving to, and supporting others

6. **Variety:** the need for the unknown, change, and new stimuli

In your quest to move an audience closer to your cause, how many of these elements do you consider when preparing a speech? When listening to other presentations, can you identify these forces at work? And do you formulate your speeches and presentations with these essential ingredients in mind?

We change our clothes, eat different foods, and watch different television shows, all in the pursuit of variety. We strive to avoid monotony, recognizing just how punishing it can be. Yet we reduce much of our speech communication to buzz words and bullet points. Your audience is too polite to say how disengaged they really are.

Far too often, speakers forget to infuse their speeches with a human element, what Tony Robbins notes in his six fundamental needs. We have become obsessed with pointing up to our PowerPoint slides and don't pay sufficient attention to forging lasting bonds with our audience. How do we solve this problem?

THE PROMISE AND CURSE OF POWERPOINT

On August 30, 2012, *Bloomberg Business Week* published an article called "Death to PowerPoint." While reading the piece, I was particularly drawn to one of its key findings:

> *"Since Microsoft launched the slide show program twenty-two years ago, it's been installed on no fewer than one billion computers; an estimated 350 PowerPoint presentations are given each second across the globe; the software's users continue to prove that no field of human endeavor can defy its facility for reducing complexity and nuance to bullet points and big ideas to tacky clip art. As with anything so ubiquitous and relied upon, PowerPoint has bred its share of contempt."*

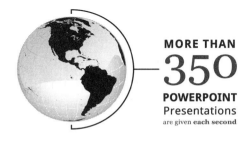

MORE THAN
350
POWERPOINT
Presentations
are given **each second**

Three years later, the number of presentations on any given weekday exceeds thirty million.

What exactly is going on? The conventional approach to Power-Point needs a massive readjustment. Many presenters go through the motions and hope that somehow they will connect, persuade, and move an audience closer to their cause.

The technologies themselves are not the problem. PowerPoint, Prezi, or Keynote do not fail to persuade. PowerPoint is just a crutch, which is frequently used ineffectively. PowerPoint could be one of our best assets—but we don't use it as well as we could. We tend to do what feels safe.

However, we depend on it because it offers great promise. It can be a graphically rich tool for visualizing information that supports your key assertions. Unfortunately, many speakers shower all their attention—their eyes, their focus, their time—on their PowerPoint slides while giving a speech instead of doing what they're really there to achieve: bond with their audience.

PowerPoint slides were never designed to be the star of the show. You are the start of the show. The audience is the star of the show. The technology you select is a supporting player, not the marquee attraction.

In our quest to communicate a large swath of facts and figures in a short time frame, we too stuff slides with text and then simply read them, word for word, aloud to our listeners. Some speakers even keep their back to the audience while they recite the words on the slides.

How, then, do we use visual aids to reinforce the messages we aim to convey?

It starts by communicating a story that is compelling, persuasive, and contains a call to action. No visual or software program can do that for you. Assuming you are ready with an engaging story, these are my "can't-fail" rules for slide shows and visual aides:

1. **Keep it simple.** Clutter kills! There should be plenty of "white space." Avoid overfilling your slides. Be mindful not to load the presentation with busy, wordy, or complicated text. Include only what is essential to support your slide's message. Less is more to minimize distractions.

   When I was in graduate school there was a political science professor who put the entire text of the Constitution on a slide to introduce the Declaration of Independence. He expected his students to read every word. A more effective approach would have been to display key concepts and words to spark discussion and engagement. He used ten minutes to communicate what could have been conveyed in a fraction of that time.

2. **Minimize bullet points and text.** Use three bullet points per slide, avoid complete sentences. The purpose of bullets is to present a talking point. However, the best slides have *no text*. Many speakers, in their desire "not to forget anything," stuff entire sentences into each bullet. When their speech is over, they breathe a sigh of relief that they "remembered to say everything." Avoid that strategy. *Don't let trying to be perfect be the enemy of the very good.* If you forgot to say something, your audience will never know it.

3. **Animate your visuals.** This is a controversial topic among speech coaches, who offer their clients varying approaches. While PowerPoints should minimize text and use visuals to support their story, I stand firm in my conviction to animate your visuals as your slide message unfolds. It is ineffective to give all your visuals away before you've had a chance to explain them in sequence. We narrate our stories in increments. Display your visuals with that same mind-set, and layer your points into the presentation one at a time.

It's helpful to fade in your images as you guide the audience to your next visual. While there are dozens of ways to "animate" an image, most of the time I use two fades: Blinds and Checkerboard. They are uncomplicated, easy-to-follow transitions that seem more natural than some of the more dramatic animation choices, like Spinner, Rise Up, or Boomerang, which often prove too distracting.

4. **Use high-quality graphics.** Many presenters use low-quality photos that are often challenging for the audience to comprehend. That can diminish the power of your talk. Keep the images clear and easy to read.

Color templates bring emotion to your story. We watch color TV and see colors in nature. Our eyes prefer contrast, variety, and depth. Black-and-white PowerPoints are contrary to the way we are accustomed to seeing objects. It's a form of nonverbal communication and is a universal language that conveys a mood or feeling. According to research:

- Color visuals increase willingness to read and increase motivation and participation by up to 80 percent.

- It enhances learning and improves retention by more than 75 percent.

- Color in advertising outsells black and white by 88 percent.[16]

Use color templates to set the tone. For instance, yellow is often associated with happiness and warmth. Orange is cheerful and confident. Green is healthy. In the USA, red, white, and blue are great choices. Patriotic and easily contrastable, these are colors that most Americans identify with and feel some level of kinship. When in Italy, use green, white, and red, the colors of the Italian flag. Use specific colors to

16   "The Power of Color in Presentations." 3M United States. http://www.3rd-force.org/meetingnetwork/readingroom/meetingguide_power_color.html.

prompt a positive association, which will heighten your audience's attention span. Choose colors wisely to persuade and motivate.

5. **Use effective charts.** Your charts have a story waiting to be told. It's important to present the data. Some professions like finance or biotechnology are data driven and can be overwhelming in the amount of analysis that needs to be presented. However, resist the impulse to overwhelm the audience with too many metrics. Instead, consider what the numbers are saying. "Apple's market share went from five to eleven percent in the last nine years." It's reasonable to start dissecting the numbers. Be mindful, however, to quickly communicate the implications of those figures.

6. **Choose fonts carefully.** There is no absolute choice. The font you choose should be seen clearly from the back of the room. For the best presenters, fonts communicate subtle messages and highlight your sense of style. Use the same font throughout your entire presentation and no more than two complementary fonts if you like some variation. Otherwise, it's difficult to follow and confusing to the audience. I tend to use Garamond, Perpetual Titling, and Calisto, as they are easy to read. However, font style is a matter of preference as long as it is legible to the audience.

7. **Use video and audio.** Use video and audio to increase cognitive processing. People learn in a variety of ways. Video and audio provide audiences a break, while allowing you to introduce another texture or medium— anything to continue the drive for variety and audience engagement. I'm a big fan, for example, of using certain

songs to communicate a message. In my desire to provoke an organization to transform its culture, I once played Michael Jackson's "Man in the Mirror": "If you want to make the world a better place, take a look at yourself, and make that . . . change." This was meant to reinforce the notion that individuals are capable of accepting responsibility for their behaviors and changing their corporate culture one person at a time. They were inspired, uplifted, and felt they were capable of helping others to change. It was consistent with the entire theme of the speech and left them humming the song in a great mood, contemplating what they could do to contribute to the firm's transformation.

REVOLUTIONIZING PERSUASIVE PRESENTATIONS WITH POWTOON

The remarkable success of Tumblr, Pinterest, and Instagram proves that a picture truly is worth a thousand words. Yet the ways in which we present pictures and images to audiences has not kept pace with the dynamic world of social media.

Instead of always depending upon the old standby, PowerPoint, it's essential to look to alternatives that can increase the visual richness of the presentation. After all, 65 percent of humans absorb more information visually than they do orally.[17] These days, audiences have become so accustomed to seeing bland PowerPoint presentations that their eyes tend to glaze over at the very mention of the word.

---

17 Mind Tools, 1998, https://www.mindtools.com/mnemlsty.html.

If you want your speech to be remembered, for it to be impactful and persuasive, find ways to display your slides with movement and energy. There are plenty of different apps and programs worth exploring, but many have found success with a user-friendly and intuitive presentation program software called PowToon. It allows speakers with no technical or design skills the ability to create engaging animated presentations.

Founded in 2012, PowToon did what so many other start-ups tried but failed to get right. The company disrupted the status quo and created a presentation category that responds to the way we absorb information in the modern age. We can now create a presentation cartoon mashup called a PowToon. If you haven't seen a PowToon in a business meeting, it's a matter of time before you do. They bring flair to your presentation with visuals that are engaging, captivating, and fun.

You don't have to produce Powtoons for every meeting or occasion. Adjust your presentation style to fit the way Millennials listen, learn, and absorb information. When preparing for a presentation, try recasting your approach. Minimize words, maximize imagery, and try including some PowToon tactics into your presentations.

To direct an audience to keep paying attention, words on the screen can be of minimal value. I find it most effective to create a vision of what I'm proposing so that it will benefit the audience. If you want viewers to pay attention with the logical part of their brains, use words, but if you want to trigger emotions to persuade, use images. If you want to fully engage viewers, create images that are lively, captivating, and memorable to get the full impact of both the logical and emotional sides of your argument.

Years ago, Walt Disney proved that converting still pages into colorful movement significantly increases our capacity to comprehend a story. Fast forward a few decades and look at how ubiquitous animation has become in our world. We watch movies. We play video games and spend a colossal amount of time absorbing photos on social media. On television, adults watch *The Simpsons* and *South Park*, which validates our appreciation for animated story telling.

Next time you're assembling a presentation, consider how the Millenials learn and keep the words off your presentation software. This new world we're selling into demands that our presentation skills stay as fresh and creative as the social media sites that command millions of views every day. We learned a lot from watching how these sites adapt to the changing world. We, too, need to change and start animating our own visuals for riveting, exciting, and persuasive presentations.

Whether you employ PowToon in your slides or not, remember these central ideas when using PowerPoint. Every performing art form—whether it's a speech, a dance, or a play—uses tools and techniques to achieve three essential goals:

1. Maintain a disciplined approach.

2. Control the flow of information.

3. Keep the practitioner and audience engaged in such a way that the experience is mutually beneficial. A speaker and listener are partners in an extended conversation. How do we best use all our senses to maximize the communication experience?

Haig Kouyoumdjian, Ph.D., is a clinical psychologist who focuses his research on innovative teaching methods. In an article in *Psychology Today*, he states, "A large body of research indicates that visual cues help us to better retrieve and remember information. The research outcomes on visual learning make complete sense when you consider that our brain is mainly an image processor, not a word processor. In fact, the part of the brain used to process words is quite small in comparison to the part that processes visual images. Words are abstract and rather difficult for the brain to retain, whereas visuals are concrete and, as such, more easily remembered."[18] His research does not recommend the elimination of text. He encourages us to continually refine our approach to find symmetry of words and visual images that resonate with the audience.

You can learn a lot about finding the right combination of words and visuals from the world's great filmmakers. Released in 1941, the movie *Citizen Kane* took a fresh and sophisticated approach to this art form. The rich visual scenes, performances, and experimental innovations in photography and sound make it one of cinema's most-admired classics. It integrated a great story with a visual style that was ahead of its time. As a communications coach, I am most enthralled by how well it integrates words with powerful yet simple images that an audience can easily absorb.

Orson Welles, the film's director, provided continual insights on the art of communication. He had the courage to create art that was powerful and distinct. Also admired for his outstanding oratory and presentation skills, I once read an interview with him that offered valuable enouragement and advice.

---

18   Kouyoumdjian, Haig, PhD. "Learning Through Visuals." Psychology Today. July 20, 2012. https://www.psychologytoday.com/blog/get-psyched/201207/learning-through-visuals.

When asked how speakers could more effectively persuade an audience, he said something powerful and applicable in any era. As you continue to develop and polish your skills, tap into Welles's energy and timeless advice: "Create your own style . . . let it be unique for yourself and yet identifiable for others."[19]

---

19   Robert RJ Schermann, "Finding Your Own Personal Style #3: Create Your Own Visual Style," *Lifehack*, http://www.lifehack.org/articles/lifestyle/finding-your-personal-style-lesson-3.html.

CHAPTER 10

Vary the Pitch: Stand and Deliver the Unexpected

"The hour of delivery is the "supreme, inevitable hour" for the orator. It is this fact that makes lack of adequate preparation such impertinence. And it is this that sends such thrills of indescribable joy through the orator's whole being when he has achieved a success—it is like the mother forgetting her pangs for the joy of bringing a son into the world."

—J. Berg Esenwein, professor of English and literature at the Pennsylvania Military College[20]

T ry throwing a ball with your right and left hand simultaneously with equal force. Now try to talk and listen at the same time. Unless your powers of coordination are extraordinary, both of these tasks will be awkward if not totally ineffective.

---

20   "A Popular Treatise On The Nature, Preparation, And Delivery Of Public Discourse," January 5, 1902.

Some neuroscientists go so far as to say our brains are incapable of doing two things at once. One will always lead the other in rapid succession. Our attention simply shifts from one movement to the next. It's no different in our modern world when someone says, "I'm multitasking." The truth is, they're not. They are doing one thing and then shifting to the other, diminishing their capacity to do them both equally well.

Similar tenets apply to speech communication. While listening to a speech, our minds lose their grip on one idea the moment our attention is diverted to another.

Many public speakers lose the attention of their listeners because they say one thing while trying to formulate the next. Their concentration trails off, causing them to start out strong, only to continue with a weak, wavering follow-up thought. Like the tail of a comet, the force and appeal of their ideas slowly begin to diminish.

When you are delivering one sentence, don't think about what follows. It's not always as easy as it sounds. The former merely informs; the latter goes beyond. In other words, focus your concentration on *speaking*. Don't try to anticipate what's ahead of you.

As you learned in chapter 7, emphatic and emotionally charged words should come at the end of a sentence. They should close out your thought and lead to your call to action. They are typically the last things listeners remember.

To be effective on center stage, link strong ideas with assertive expressions. Concentrate your full attention on delivering your points with concentrated power, purpose, and passion. If your attention is divided, the attention of your audience will be as well.

To divide your attention is to divide your power. Divide the power and you diminish your capacity.

PAUSES, PRESENTATIONS, AND VIDEOTAPE

As you learned in chapter 8, remember to integrate strategic pauses into your speeches to heighten the power of your delivery. A pause offers an opportunity for transitions. Deliver one thought at a time in ways that ensure your sentences have equal force from beginning to end. Like delivering a knockout punch, focus your energy on one target and then deliver it. Concentrate, consolidate, and mobilize your power. Pause for effect. Then *speak.*

Also try not to be mechanical in your delivery, using expressions that lack nuance or force. If you listen to unskilled actors, lawyers, or speakers, they tend to rant incoherently or employ a robotic cadence, offering merely a collection of sounds painfully strung together to look, feel, and sound like communication. That's not effective communication; it's just talking.

Your vocal delivery—i.e., how you present your speech—will influence how your audience hears your message. You cannot persuade others if you don't speak in a way that engages, transforms, or moves them closer to your cause.

When working with my clients, I often videotape their speeches so they can watch themselves. I focus on their delivery—how they look and sound to analyze both their body language and their voice. This is how they learn to become better speakers; seeing is believing. Watching oneself "perform" is one of the most challenging exercises in self-awareness. It's not easy to be pushed outside of your comfort zone and be forced to see yourself as you truly are—flaws and all.

But the amount of wisdom that can be gained from these sessions is profound.

"I had no idea I did that," my clients will tell me. "I twirl my hair? Rock back and forth? Put my hands in my pockets?"

I identify where my clients need improvement and then work on delivery, especially in terms of their *pitch* and *pacing*.

What is pitch exactly? It's the relative position of a vocal tone: high, medium, or low. There are many variations. We apply pitch not only to a single word but also as an exclamation. "WOW!" "STOP!" "HEADS UP!" Great communicators apply pitch at different moments throughout a speech, thus minimizing any chance of monotony by infusing their delivery with variety and unpredictability.

Every change in thought is an opportunity to change the pitch. This is one of the most violated principles in public speaking, especially when people try to memorize their speeches. They sound stilted and rehearsed.

If you want to hear how monotony sounds, try saying the same word over and over again at the same pitch. No highs, no lows, nothing to break up the boredom. Think instead of mountain peaks and valleys. This applies to volume, emphasis, pitch, pace, and more. Like a good song, we aim for highs, lows, and everything in between to keep the discussion engaging.

PERFECT PITCH: A CASE STUDY OF DAN SIMON OF VESTED, INC.

To say Dan Simon is the master's master of communication is to understate his expertise. He commands English and vocal delivery so skillfully that he earns his living transforming good communicators into great ones. Simon is CEO and cofounder of Vested, a New York-based communications consulting firm that has run campaigns for some of the biggest brands in finance, including Bloomberg, Citigroup, JP Morgan, and Citadel.

He also happens to be a personal mentor, who's been invaluable over the years in helping me to properly vary my own vocal rhythms. For Simon, great communication is all about finding the right mix of serious versus light-hearted moments, statistics and gripping human stories, as well as fast versus slow speech cadences. It's variability, he insists, that is critical to capturing and holding an audience's attention. Anything else is just monotone soliloquy on a fast track to death by PowerPoint.

Even in a world buried under an avalanche of digital communication technologies, Simon is steadfast in his conviction that all great communicators have one thing in common: they are great storytellers. What's old is new again. Whether around campfires or modern boardrooms, the best at persuasively communicating their thoughts, fears, and aspirations have done so in story form.

PowerPoint presentations are fine, Simon argues, but visual metaphors are even better. Picture a scene in ancient Egypt five thousand years ago. Two women are sitting by the banks of the Nile. One is crying because she just broke up with her boyfriend only to hear her friend say, "Don't worry, there are plenty of fish in the sea." Think about the powerful simplicity of that metaphor. Simon explains that visual metaphors are like "linguistic fractals," using imagery to condense an enormous amount of information into a concise phrase. A PowerPoint slide, no matter how artfully crafted, can never resonate as powerfully as a well-placed, well-timed visual metaphor that paints a rich image in the mind of an audience.

Speakers who are able to insert carefully crafted metaphors into their presentations are able to generate a unique rhythm that keeps people interested, but speakers also have to find ways to properly express their enthusiasm for the topic at hand. Think about Winston Churchill, for example. He was called upon to talk about extremely weighty matters, such as the very survival of Great Britain. As you'll see below, he also found a way to communicate the importance of the cause.

Simon advocates that we should all channel our own Winston Churchill from time to time. We might not be talking about the fate of Western civilization, but we can keep people interested and excited by varying the pitch, speed, and cadence of our speeches just as he did. "The content isn't going to sell itself," says Simon. "The great speakers are not always the ones with the better content. Strong delivery often compensates for weak material. An exceptional communicator gets a listener to hear financial regulation but to feel like it's the fate of Western civilization hanging in the balance. When it comes to cadence, Churchill was the master:

> *You ask what is our policy? I can say: it is to wage war, by sea, land, and air, with all our might and with all the strength that God can give us; to wage war against a monstrous tyranny, never surpassed in the dark, monumental catalogue of human crime. That is our policy.*
>
> *We shall go to the end, we shall fight in France, we shall fight on the seas and oceans, we shall fight with growing confidence*

and growing strength in the air, we shall defend our island, whatever the cost may be, we shall fight on the beaches, we shall fight on the landing grounds, we shall fight in the fields, and in the streets; we shall never surrender.

As Dan Simon always says, when great content meets great delivery, you can deliver incredibly memorable speeches that people will talk about for decades.

HOW TO DEVELOP A MUSICAL DELIVERY

What's the difference in speech delivery between a high pitch and low pitch? Think of it as the contrast between a cello and a violin. The violin sounds high and the cello low. Played together, you can hear some beautiful music. The same with high and low pitches in a series of sentences. For example, try delivering these two with varied pitches and you'll hear how these blend together to yield an effective result.

> *[High pitch] "I have to give the presentation of my life to the Executive Committee. [lower] But I don't know where to start."*

Continually changing your pitch is a necessity. Our unconscious mind does this naturally. Vocal tones rise and fall to support the emotions we seek to convey. Ask someone to give a speech, however, and some people abandon their instincts. You hear nervous tension in the form of single-pitch monotony. Avoid those traps. Change your cadence and pitch. Think like a violin and then, a cello.

One of the best ways to grab your audience's attention is to change your pace suddenly and with tremendous force. Go from low to high in an instant. For all intents and purposes, you're acting. So be it! Just go with it.

This contrast in tone arouses emotion and captures listeners' attention. *"Give me liberty* [low, pause] . . . or *GIVE ME DEATH!* [high]" Use sudden changes of pitch to add drama and suspense. You're signaling the audience with a "heads up" and forcing them to pay attention to what follows.

Likewise, you can lower the volume in the opposite direction for equal effect. Moving from high to low works as well. When used to emphasize a certain point, change the tone with a rapid transition that keeps the audience equally enthralled.

"The World Trade Center was just attacked [high]! The casualties are simply too many to count [low]."

The change in pitch from one sentence to the other works in opposition: They complement each other to achieve a desired effect.

"Change the pace." "Up the tempo." "Double time."

These are commands a music teacher uses when teaching others to play an instrument. Surrounded by musicians growing up, I heard those words all the time. Teachers were obsessed about the rate of movement, as measured by the time required to execute a specific note or set of notes. This training helped me become a better speaker later in life.

Public speaking is a lot like learning to play an instrument. Like many vocalists, it takes years of training, dedication, and a great coach to master the fundamentals. It takes longer to sing a whole note than a quarter note. Consequently, I encourage career communicators to think as musicians when ready to stand and deliver.

OVERCOMING SPEECH ANXIETY: ENDURING LESSONS FROM *THE KING'S SPEECH*

A continual change of tempo adds power to your message. Many actors assert that change of pace is a valuable technique. Study the great ones (Meryl Streep comes to mind), and listen closely to the way they speak. They can read the phone book and it will sound interesting. This change applies not only to words but to phrases, sentences, and entire sections of their speeches. The more you change the pace, pitch, and tempo, the more likely you'll drive home your key points.

Watch the 2011 movie *The King's Speech,* and you'll learn many valuable lessons.

In the film, Colin Firth plays King George VI, who, through no choice of his own, became the monarch of the United Kingdom when his brother abdicated the throne. It was 1939, and Great Britain had just declared war on Germany.

The film centers on the relationship between the new king, a stutterer, and his speech coach, Lionel Logue, played by Geoffrey Rush. Part of King George's responsibility was to speak to his subjects live through a relatively new device at that time called the radio. Terrified at the need to connect with his subjects, he would have preferred to live in the shadows. However, in wartime England, silence was not an option. The king of the world's oldest monarchy needed to be seen—and *heard.* The British people wanted to know that their king supported their efforts to fight in World War II and rid the world of the evil lurking across the English Channel.

Fearing the embarrassment and shame of his debilitating stutter, King George felt defeated from the onset. He was painfully aware that if he didn't confront his fears, he would be crushed under the weight of his countrymen's expectations.

I see a lot of King George VI in some of my clients. While most don't have the same physical challenges to overcome, they often fall into a handful of missteps that weaken their stage presence. When asked to present something forcefully, they feel inadequate. They can't seem to shake off the nervous tension that erodes their confidence and inhibits their success.

When you watch the finale of the movie, you see King George in a studio about to broadcast his first major wartime speech on the radio. Nervous and looking as if he were heading toward his own execution, he faces the challenge of his life head on. Standing next to him is his coach.

His teacher stands confident, looking dapper in a tuxedo, and ready to watch his client, the King of England, stand and deliver. With the second movement of Beethoven's "Seventh Symphony" playing in the background, we see the coach and protégé in action. The King spoke; the coach conducted.

By varying the pitch and pace, word for word, the king delivers a masterful speech at a moment in time when both men had so much to gain or lose from his performance. Millions of British citizens stood ready to hear their King speak firmly to unify the nation in its fight against the Axis powers.

The King of England learned to exceed his own expectations in the face of adversity. He demonstrated that there is hope for anyone who chooses to confront his or her own fears as well. King George is an inspiration for everyone looking to climb the career ladder of success.

Watch the finale, pay attention to the King's words, and think about their meaning. While they're about the war, they are also about facing his flaws as a speaker and finding the courage and discipline to overcome them. There are a multitude of lessons in this speech for all of us, if we're only willing to see and internalize them.

So let go. Strive for progress, not perfection. Succumb to nature's natural forces, and let your unconscious mind do the talking. The King did, and so can you!

In this grave hour, perhaps the most fateful in our history, I send to every household of my peoples, both at home and overseas, this message, spoken with the same depth of feeling for each one of you as if I were able to cross your threshold and speak to you myself. For the second time in the lives of most of us, we are at war.

We have been forced into a conflict, for we are called, with our allies, to meet the challenge of a principle which, if it were to prevail, would be fatal to any civilized order in the world.

I ask them to stand calm and firm and united in this time of trial.

The task will be hard. There may be dark days ahead, and war can no longer be confined to the battlefield, but we can only do the right as we see the right, and reverently commit our cause to God.

If one and all we keep resolutely faithful to it, ready for whatever service or sacrifice it may demand, then with God's help, we shall prevail.

Public speaking for many people is a monumental struggle—and a frustrating internal conflict. I acknowledge there is fear and danger inherent in taking on that struggle. The stakes can be high when you're alone, facing a vast crowd of unfamiliar faces. But, when you want to take that next big step in your career, take a moment to analyze the importance of communication. You'll appreciate that self-improvement pays off in unexpected ways.

I see some of myself in Geoffrey Rush's character. Clients come to me with challenges to overcome in pursuit of meeting their goals. Although each situation is unique, we climb this mountain together. My mission is to help everyone to exceed their own expectations and transform them into the communicators they believe they're capable of becoming.

As the king says, the task shall be hard. And there will be dark days and moments when you feel like you won't be up to the task. But if you stay faithful and commit to your professional development, you'll prevail in the end. You will advance and grow more confident in ways that are beyond even your own expectations.

Conclusion

eo Tolstoy, the Russian novelist, famously wrote, "Everyone thinks of changing the world, but no one thinks of changing himself." Tolstoy's pronouncement is a useful starting point for any businessperson committed to climbing their way to the top. If you expect to move others closer to your cause, move yourself to a place you've never been.

By learning, practicing, and refining the Ten Commandments of Great Communicators, you made a conscious decision to invest in yourself. When opportunity knocks and it's time to stand and deliver, it's also time for self-development. We climb mountains and learn to persuasively communicate not because it's easy but because it's hard. Confronting the challenges and working though these struggles help us determine who we truly are.

The individuals I coach who transform into great communicators and extraordinary leaders have one thing in common: a keen sense of self-awareness. To be self-aware and translate that understanding into success is easier said than done. Getting started is usually the hardest part. To master these skills requires interactivity, experiential learning, and some patience. Like an athlete, it's important to have a mentor or coach who can uncover your blind spots and provide the feedback necessary for sustained improvement.

I am blessed with the opportunity to help others with their career ascents. It's a pleasure to watch them evolve, mature, and become the kind of leaders they aspire to be. Their career trajectories are not miracles. It comes through hard work, being open to feedback, and lots of practice.

Edmund Hillary didn't hesitate in his quest for the summit of Mount Everest. Despite the enormity of his achievement, he regards himself and his partner Tenzing Norgay as hardworking men, not heroes. While he wouldn't have reached the top without such technical competence, he admired the human drive to understand, explore, and overcome giant obstacles in the face of adversity. He set a goal, took one step at a time, and collaborated with Norgay to climb to the top. He also relied on the Law of Reciprocity to help others in his quest for success. Asked about his mind-set and motivation in spite of the hardship, his response was as clear as it was inspiring. "Aim high. There is very little virtue in easy victory."

As you practice and refine the Ten Commandments, seek inspiration from the great climbers and communicators. As you ascend to your career summit, internalize the following call to action from writer and lyricist Paulo Cohelo, "Make a promise: Now that you have discovered a force that you were not even aware of, tell yourself that from now on you will use this force for the rest of your days. Promise yourself to discover another mountain, and set off on another adventure."

Thank you for joining me on this climb. It's been an honor to be your guide.

About the Author

Chuck Garcia is founder of Climb Leadership Consulting and a Professor of Organizational Leadership at Mercy College in New York. He coaches executives on public speaking, sales skills, and leadership development. A twenty-five-year veteran of Wall Street, he spent fourteen years in sales and marketing at Bloomberg in a variety of leadership positions. He was Director of Business Development at BlackRock Solutions, an arm of the world's largest investment-management firm, and was a Managing Director at Citadel, an alternative investment-management firm.

He is a mountaineer and has climbed some of the world's tallest peaks, including Mount Kilimanjaro, Mount Elbrus, the Matterhorn, and mountains in Alaska and the Andes.

Chuck is available for speaking, coaching, and training development. He can be reached at:

chuck@climbleadership.com

Climb Leadership Consulting

10 Habitat Lane | Cortlandt Manor, NY 10567

www.aclimbtothetop.com | www.climbleadership.com

https://www.linkedin.com/in/chuck-garcia-015128

Resources

THE TEN COMMANDMENTS
OF GREAT PRESENTATIONS

1 **PRIMARY/RECENCY EFFECT**
People remember the first and last thing you say. Make the open and close count!

2 **EMOTIONAL APPEAL**
People buy on emotion and support that decision with logic. Present the facts...with enthusiasm and passion.

3 **SPEAK WITH CONVICTION**
If you speak with weak, wavering words...you can't convince them because you are not convinced yourself.

4 **BODY LANGUAGE**
Most of your communication is non-verbal. Be mindful of what you don't say and how you don't say it!

5 **MINIMIZE THE DISTANCE**
Don't stand behind a podium or anywhere that inhibits your connection with the audience.

6 **SPEAK IN THE RULE OF 3**
Life, liberty, and the pursuit of happiness. Your listeners can only absorb three concepts at a time.

7 **SPEAKER PUNCTUATES**
Be sure to exclaim and underscore your main points.

8 **PAUSE POWER**
Mark Twain said, "The right word may be effective, but no word was ever as effective as a well timed pause."

9 **ANIMATE YOUR VISUALS**
Don't overload PowerPoint with words. Animate each point, allowing listeners to absorb your information.

10 **VARY THE PITCH**
Speed, cadence, and delivery to keep it lively!

CLIMB LEADERSHIP
—CONSULTING—

Chuck Garcia | Chuck@ClimbLeadership.com | 917.348.8264

10 ENHANCE YOUR SPEECH

WAYS TO

1 DISTINCTION

There is something about you that makes you different from others. You are **bold** or *italic*, but never ordinary.
Your passion and energy are contagious.

2 IT'S NOT ABOUT YOU

Replace ego with empathy and shift the focus from "I" to "you." You develop the topic considering the audiences concerns and what they are capable of absorbing.

3 EASY TO FOLLOW

Your simple and concise approach trumps complicated and confusing every time.

4 SITUATIONAL AWARENESS

You read an audience well and know when to dial it up, dial it down, and dial it off! You adjust easily to unexpected changes.

5 A PICTURE'S WORTH 1000 WORDS

50% of your presentation's impact is visual. Your colorful, well-designed images convey positive feelings that stay in the hearts and minds of your audience.

6 BE POETIC

You choose the right words, at the right time, in the right order.

7 CONFIDENT AND AT EASE

You channel any nervous energy to deliver an exciting and compelling speech.

8 LOOK AND SOUND

You are dressed for the occasion and use hands, eye contact, and body language to communicate effectively. With no "ums" and "likes" you minimize distractions. You give each listener the feeling of personal, one to one communication.

9 YOU CARE

You give your audience opportunities to register their opinions, pause for questions, and show appreciation for their engagement. You help them to consider something that resonates long after your speech is over.

10 CALL TO ACTION

You have instructed and inspired the audience in such a way as to provoke a reaction. Given the value you added to their lives, you left them feeling as if they want to be a part of your community. Whatever you are selling, they are buying!

CLIMB LEADERSHIP
—CONSULTING—

10 CALM YOUR NERVES

WAYS TO

1 AN EXTENDED CONVERSATION

The presentation is nothing more than an extended conversation. Rely on the familiarity of your subject matter to put you at ease. You're the expert. Most people in the audience are not.

2 VISUALIZATION IS KEY

Visualize what you want the experience to be prior to stepping on stage. Adjust accordingly if things don't seem as you expected. Some of the best speeches I've seen went off-script and were improvised.

3 DON'T WORRY

Don't worry about the things you can't control. Unproductive worrying sucks the energy you need to stay focused on your energetic and compelling presentation.

4 KEEP MOVING

Don't stop for mistakes. The odds are good that no one will notice your error. Keep talking.

5 FORGIVE AND FORGET

Don't punish yourself for things you may have forgotten. The audience will never know what you meant to include.

6 WATCH YOUR AUDIENCE

Watch the audience and how they react. Remember that great speakers have a heightened sense of situational awareness. Make immediate adjustments in response to the room dynamic.

7 FORGET THE NOTES

Forget the notes you wanted to keep in your hand. They are a crutch and get in the way. They break your rhythm by looking down and up too much. Look at your audience... all the time.

8 ELIMINATE BARRIERS

Eliminate any barriers. Stay as close to your audience as possible. It is difficult to establish rapport from a distance.

9 LOOSEN THE TENSION

Bend your knees and/or stretch your arms to loosen the tension. It is best to step on stage after the body is warmed up. This isn't that different from exercise.

10 BE PREPARED

Don't wait until the last minute. Never wing it! Feeling unprepared is a huge source of anxiety. It's inexcusable and can cause serious self-inflicted harm.

CLIMB LEADERSHIP
—CONSULTING—

10 CHANGE YOUR
WAYS TO **ATTITUDE**

1 INTERPRET YOUR FEELINGS

Accept the fact that your body is preparing for a challenge. Use the energy created for productive purposes to compose and deliver the presentation.

2 DEVELOP YOUR SKILLS

You feel comfortable doing things you do well, less comfortable doing things you don't do well. The more you are pushed out of your comfort zone the quicker you'll adjust to the most demanding circumstances.

3 SET REALISTIC GOALS

Stop demanding that everything be perfect. Strive for progress, not perfection! One step at a time.

4 SELF-CONFIDENCE

Keep telling yourself you are either a terrible or a great presenter. Either way, you're guaranteed to be right!

5 PRACTICE AT REGULAR INTERVALS

Several short presentations are much better conditioning than one or two long ones.

6 OVERCOME CHALLENGES

Everyone has weaknesses. You can't fix all of them all the time. You can however, compensate for them. Choose the order to address them; and fix it!

7 THINK POSITIVE

We all talk to ourselves. What do you say to the person in the mirror? There is no failure, only feedback. Stay positive and good things happen.

8 TAKE IT FOR A TEST RUN

When preparing, try out your speech in front of 3 people you trust to provide constructive criticism. The adjustments made will not only improve the presentation but boost your confidence.

9 REMIND YOURSELF

Your success doesn't happen by chance – but by choice. Your choice!

10 YOU DON'T STAY THE SAME

You either get better or worse! Choose wisely!

CLIMB LEADERSHIP
CONSULTING

INCREASE YOUR CHANCES
TO GET THE SALE

GOAL   **IMPORTANCE**   **CARE**

What do I need the audience to think, feel, or do in order to accomplish my goal? Why is should they care?

WORDS   **BEARING**   **ENGAGEMENT**

Your audience immediately begins to form impressions... and assesses you in the vocabulary of personal judgments.

INSPIRATION   **PERSUASION**   **PROVOCATION**

If you expect to move someone to your cause, you'll need all three. Your mission is to change someone's mind, heart, and provoke a call to action.

Recommended Reading

There are many excellent books on career development, leadership, and communication. Here are a few I recommend:

1. *Strengths Finder 2.0*, by Tom Rath

I give a copy of this book to every client and student. It helps me understand what makes them tick, and it is a great tool for their self-awareness.

2. *The Power of Communication: Skills to Build Trust, Inspire Loyalty, and Lead Effectively*, by Helio Fred Garcia

The Power of Communication builds on the US Marine Corps' legendary publication, *Warfighting,* showing how to apply the Corps' proven leadership and strategy doctrine to all forms of public communication—and achieve truly extraordinary results.

3. *The Hard Truth About Soft Skills: Workplace Lessons Smart People Wish They'd Learned Sooner*, by Peggy Klaus

Soft skills are finally earning the respect they deserve. Learn to master these skills to help you continue your career climb.

4. *How to Win Friends and Influence People*, by Dale Carnegie.

Published in 1936, this is a classic and should be on every leader's shelf. The lessons are timeless and still relevant.

5. *How to Master the Art of Selling,* by Tom Hopkins

This was my professional development bible. Although I first read it thirty-five years ago, the sales tactics and techniques are as applicable today as then.

6. *To Sell is Human: The Surprising Truth About Persuading, Convincing and Influencing Others,* by Dan Pink

I'm a fan of all Dan Pink's books, but this one resonated the most. I recommend it for anyone contemplating a career in sales or marketing.

7. *YES, AND: Lessons from The Second City,* by Kelly Leonard and Tom Yorton.

This book helps us understand and put into action the art of improvisation. Thinking on your feet is an important skill set that can be developed. It also helps us to understand the power of ensembles to create innovative and inspirational work.

8. *Creativity, Inc.: Overcoming the Unseen Forces That Stand in the Way of True Inspiration,* by Ed Catmull

Learn how Pixar turns ideas into powerful and creative works of art. The leadership lessons are priceless.

9. *Emotional Intelligence 2.0,* by Travis Bradberry and Jean Greaves.

This is a great book to learn about the importance of EQ in the work place and in your personal life.

10. *The Charge: Activacting the 10 Human Drives That Make You Feel Alive* by Brendon Burchard.

An informative and inspiring guide to help us understand how to keep our internal charge alive to lead a happy, healthy, and prosperous life.

Reach a New Peak in Your Career!

Visit **www.aclimbtothetop.com** to help launch your career to new heights.

Free Resources: Go to www.aclimbtothetop.com to access tools and materials to help your business's leaders follow the steps in this book toward achieving their goals.

Speaking Engagements: Give your audience the opportunity to transform your corporate culture in an interactive setting with the author of this book, and learn actionable tips and tools to inspire, persuade, and provoke change. Visit **www.aclimbtothetop. com** for more information.

Career Assessment: If you, your family, or coworkers in your organization are interested in a private consultation with the author, visit **www.aclimbtothetop.com** for more information.